The Metropolitan Museum of Art

Notable Acquisitions

1965–1975

The Metropolitan Museum of Art

ON THE COVER:

Hans Hofmann (1880–1966), American

Rhapsody, oil on canvas, 1965

84¼ x 60½ in.

Gift of Renate Hofmann, 1975

Designed by Peter Oldenburg with Arlene Goldberg
Type set by Custom Composition Company, Inc., York, Pennsylvania
Printed by The Leether Press, Boston
Bound by Robert Burlen & Son, Inc., Hingham, Massachusetts

LIBRARY OF CONGRESS CATALOGING IN PUBLICATION DATA

New York (City). Metropolitan Museum of Art.

The Metropolitan Museum of Art: notable acquisitions, 1965–1975.

1. Art—New York (City)—Catalogs. 2. New York (City).
Metropolitan Museum of Art.

N610.A6745   708'.1471   75–31761
ISBN 0-87099-141-8

Contents

Foreword

Collecting is the lifeblood of the Metropolitan. From its myriad collections, spanning five thousand years and illustrating most of the known civilizations of history, spring all the significant functions of the Museum: education, communication, scholarship, preservation, and exhibition. Curiously enough, the mission of collecting has not up to now been explained to our public in all its complexities; that is the principal purpose of the exhibition *Patterns of Collecting.* Through it, Olga Raggio, Chairman of Western European Arts and the organizer of the show, has indicated why we collect specific works of art and how they came into the collections. The exhibition, and the present catalogue, are tributes to the extraordinary connoisseurship of the curatorial staff—their acumen, sensitivity, knowledge, and courage.

THOMAS HOVING
Director

Preface

Between 1965 and 1975 more than fifteen thousand works of art were added to the holdings of the Metropolitan Museum. And this number does not include costumes, prints, the Robert Lehman Collection, and the collection of the Museum of Primitive Art, which will come to us with the opening of the Michael C. Rockefeller Wing.

These many works, representing five millennia of mankind's artistic endeavor, have entered the Museum as gifts and bequests or as purchases from special or general acquisitions funds. By far the largest number—about eighty-five percent— are the result of the generosity of friends and benefactors who have donated or bequeathed the works they themselves lovingly collected.

The following summary catalogue describes a selection of about thirteen hundred works chosen by seventeen curatorial departments as the most important and representative objects added to their collections during the last decade. The publication accompanies *Patterns of Collecting,* an exhibition of about one-third of the works of art included here. The exhibition is designed to present many of the pieces for the first time and also to illustrate the many ways in which the growth of an encyclopaedic museum must be understood.

Because of the obvious space limitations the many collections that have recently become part of the Museum are represented by only a few token items in both the catalogue and the exhibition. Two such collections are that of Irwin Untermyer, which has brought us over two thousand works of European decorative arts, and the Lesley and Emma Sheafer Collection, so rich in important examples of German furniture, porcelain, and silver. Nor has the Robert Lehman Collection been included in this selection, since a special guidebook to the Lehman wing has just been published.

The arrangement of the entries by departments reflects the curatorial structure of the Museum. Within each department the objects have been grouped by categories and then listed by year of accession, indicated in abbreviated fashion by the first digits of the accession number. The only exceptions to this arrangement are the entries submitted by the Department of American Paintings and Sculpture, the American Wing, the Department of Far Eastern Art, and The Costume Institute, where, because of the homogeneity of the material, chronological order seemed preferable.

Among the works that came to the Museum as gifts and bequests, those designated by an accession number earlier than 1965 were partial or life interest gifts that actually entered the collections in the course of the last ten years. In another special category is a group of Egyptian papyri, 22.3.516-528. These have been included because, although they have been in the Museum since 1922, they have only recently been deciphered and properly identified.

The format of this publication is intended primarily to provide a compact illustrated listing, but the brief comments by the curatorial staff often go beyond that function—to suggest why an object was deemed of sufficient importance to be added to our collections.

My warmest thanks go to all those throughout the Museum who have so expertly and willingly given me continuous help and cooperation in fulfilling my task of organizing this catalogue and the exhibition.

OLGA RAGGIO
Chairman, Western European Arts

American Paintings and Sculpture

Comments by   Lewis I. Sharp, Assistant Curator

Henry Benbridge
  1743–1812

Portrait of an Unknown Gentleman
  Oil on canvas
  49¼ x 39½ in.
  Morris K. Jesup Fund, Maria DeWitt Jesup
   Fund, and Louis V. Bell Fund, 69.202

Benbridge, a sophisticated and "Europeanized"
Philadelphia portraitist and miniaturist, was one
of America's leading painters of the late eighteenth century. This portrait was probably painted
in the early 1770s, shortly after the artist had
studied with Pompeo Batoni and Raphael Mengs
in Rome and Benjamin West in London. Benbridge's oils are rare, and this unusually fine example strengthens the collection in the area of
mid-Atlantic portraiture.

Matthew Pratt
  1734–1805

Cadwallader Colden and Warren DeLancey
  Oil on canvas
  50 x 39⅞ in.
  Morris K. Jesup Fund, 69.76

This large and rare double portrait, beautiful as
well as historically valuable, was painted about
1775, at the height of Pratt's career. Cadwallader
Colden, shown with his grandson, was an important colonial politician and intellectual leader.

John Durand
Active 1766–1782

Richard Crossfield
Oil on canvas
50¼ x 34½ in.
Gift of Edgar William and Bernice Chrysler Garbisch, 69.279.2

Durand was an untrained itinerant portrait painter known to have worked in New York, Virginia, and Connecticut. *Richard Crossfield,* one of his few known full-length portraits, has a crispness of outline and rich coloristic passages that rank it with his finest works. Another of many gifts of Edgar William and Bernice Chrysler Garbisch that have strengthened the Museum's collection in the area of early American portraiture.

Gilbert Stuart
1755–1828

Louis-Marie, Vicomte de Noailles
Oil on canvas
50 x 40 in.
Signed and dated: G. Stuart 1798
Purchase, Henry R. Luce Gift, Elihu Root, Jr., Bequest, Rogers Fund, Maria DeWitt Jesup Fund, Morris K. Jesup Fund, and Charles and Anita Blatt Gift, 1970.262

Stuart, one of America's foremost portraitists, painted this fluent, full-length portrait in 1798. The brother-in-law of Lafayette, Noailles played an important role in the Yorktown campaign and represented the French army in negotiating the surrender of Lord Cornwallis (1781).

Benjamin West
1738–1820

Moses Viewing the Promised Land
Oil on wood panel
19 x 28¾ in.
Signed and dated: B. West 1801
Gift of Mr. and Mrs. James W. Fosburgh, by exchange, 69.73

Born in Philadelphia, West moved to England and became the historical painter to George III. His London studio was a center for visiting American artists. This small, spontaneous sketch is one of thirty-six biblical subjects chosen to decorate the king's new chapel at Windsor. The powerful simplicity of the composition, dramatic handling of the light, and rich use of paint distinguish the picture as a superb example of early romantic painting.

Edward Hicks
1780–1849

Peaceable Kingdom
  Oil on canvas
  18 x 24 in.
  Gift of Edgar William and Bernice Chrysler
    Garbisch, 1970.283.1

Hicks was a Pennsylvania Quaker. His excellent sense of design and color gives his canvases a vigor and originality seldom equaled in American primitive art. This is one of a large number of important American primitive paintings given to the Museum in the last thirteen years by Edgar William and Bernice Chrysler Garbisch.

William Sidney Mount
1807–1868

Cider Making
  Oil on canvas
  27 x 34⅛ in.
  Signed, dated, and inscribed: Wm. S. Mount./
    1841; (on back) CIDER-MAKING./ Wm. S.
    Mount./1841./Painted for/C. Augt. Davis/
    N. York
  Charles Allen Munn Bequest, by exchange,
    66.126

Although regarded for a time merely as a masterful celebration of familiar rural pleasures, this work has recently revealed political overtones relating it to the rhetoric and imagery of the slogan "Log Cabin and Hard Cider" adopted by the Whigs in William Henry Harrison's successful campaign for the presidency in 1840.

Fitz Hugh Lane
1804–1865

Golden State Entering New York Harbor, 1854
  Oil on canvas
  26 x 48 in.
  Signed and dated (on back): Painted by Fitz
    H. . . Lane/Gloucester/Mass. A.D. 1854.
  Morris K. Jesup Fund, Maria DeWitt Jesup
    Fund, and Gift of Hanson K. Corning, by
    exchange, 1974.33

Lane, one of the major nineteenth-century American marine painters and a leading exponent of the "luminist" style, combines a panoramic view of the bustling marine traffic in the choppy waters of the harbor and a carefully delineated portrait of the beautiful, sleek clipper ship. This is the only example of Lane's work in the collection.

Jerome B. Thompson
1814–1886

The Belated Party on Mansfield Mountain
  Oil on canvas
  38 x 63⅛ in.
  Signed and dated: Jerome Thompson/1858
  Rogers Fund, 69.182

Thompson, although overshadowed by George Caleb Bingham and William Sidney Mount, produced some of the period's most impressive landscape-genre paintings. This large and rare example of his work combines a mood of revery with the drama and beauty of nature in an appealing romantic vision.

Francis William Edmonds
1806–1863

The New Bonnet
  Oil on canvas
  25 x 30 in.
  Signed and dated: F. W. Edmonds/1858
  Purchase, Erving Wolf Foundation Gift and Gift of Hanson K. Corning, by exchange, 1975.27.1

Edmonds, a banker by trade, was an enthusiastic and important painter of popular literary subjects and domestic life in New York in the mid-nineteenth century. In this work the stagelike composition, meticulous rendering of light, objects, and surfaces, and the overriding prosaic quality are all characteristic. The Museum's first Edmonds and an important addition to the department's limited selection of early American genre painting.

William Bradford
1823–1892

Shipwreck off Nantucket
  Oil on canvas
  40 x 64 in.
  John Osgood and Elizabeth Amis Cameron Blanchard Memorial Fund, Fosburgh Fund, Inc. Gift, and Maria DeWitt Jesup Fund, 1971.192

The American marine painter and photographer William Bradford, like the artist-explorers Frederic Church and Albert Bierstadt, was interested in capturing the dramatic aspect of exotic places and the turbulent forces of nature. Painted in about 1860, *Shipwreck off Nantucket* reveals the power of a hurricane and the tragedy of a whaling ship going down. It is one of the few major marine paintings, and the only work by Bradford, in the collection.

Samuel Colman
1832–1920

Alhambra
Oil on canvas
47½ x 71½ in.
Signed and dated: S. Colman 65.
Owned jointly by The Metropolitan Museum of
Art and Mrs. Oswald C. Hering, in memory
of her husband, 68.19

Colman, after studying briefly with the Hudson
River painter Asher B. Durand, traveled to France
and Spain. The sketches he made during the trip
provided models for later paintings, including this
beautiful large canvas, which, in its romantic
view of old Spain, combines a colorful panoramic
vista with a meticulous sense of detail.

Ralph Albert Blakelock
1847–1919

The Boulder and the Flume
Oil on canvas
54 x 28 in.
Signed: Blakelock
Gift of Mr. and Mrs. Hugh J. Grant, 1974.212

Although there is evidence of the artist's heavily
mottled style, this is an atypical canvas in that
his interest in the complex composition of the
planks running along the flume supersedes his
usual preoccupation with expressive, dreamlike
subjects. The painting is well documented, having
been in Frederick S. Gibbs's collection of Blakelock paintings until 1904, when it was acquired
by Hugh J. Grant, in whose possession it remained until it was given to the Museum.

Mary Cassatt
1844–1926

Lydia Crocheting in the Garden at Marly
Oil on canvas
26 x 37 in.
Signed: Mary Cassatt
Owned jointly by Mrs. Gardner Cassatt and
The Metropolitan Museum of Art, 65.184

Cassatt was the only American to join the group
of French artists known as the impressionists.
This beautiful, fully developed painting exemplifies the impressionists' use of luminous, high-
keyed palette, oblique vantage point, sweeping
diagonal perspective, and abrupt cropping of the
figure. A percentage of the painting was given to
the Museum in 1965 by Mrs. Gardner Cassatt, the
wife of the nephew of the artist, and yearly in-
crements continue to be made by the donor.

John Frederick Peto
1854–1907

Old Souvenirs
  Oil on canvas
  27 x 22 in.
  Falsely signed and dated (bottom, left of center): W M HARNETT./1881
  Bequest of Oliver Burr Jennings, 68.205.3

Peto's name and his oeuvre have been reestablished only since the 1940s. Prior to that many of his canvases received forged signatures of William Harnett, his more famous contemporary. In contrast to Harnett's generally lit, carefully detailed, and hard-painted subjects, Peto's canvases reveal an interest in the effects of a direct light source upon an object and a more generalized impression of soft contours.

John Henry Twachtman
1853–1902

Arques-La-Bataille
  Oil on canvas
  60 x 78⅞ in.
  Signed and dated: J. H. TWACHTMAN./1885/PARIS
  Morris K. Jesup Fund, 68.52

Twachtman was an influential member of the American impressionist group popularly called "The Ten." This work, painted in Paris in 1885, stands today as one of the masterpieces of nineteenth-century American painting. Its restricted palette, subtle tonal transitions, and strong calligraphic motifs reflect the influences of French impressionism, Japanese art, and Whistler's tonal studies.

William Merritt Chase
1849–1916

At the Seaside
  Oil on canvas
  20 x 34 in.
  Signed: Wᵐ M. Chase
  Bequest of Miss Adelaide Milton de Groot (1876–1967), 67.187.123

This canvas manifests Chase's mastery of color, texture, and dashing brushstrokes and reflects his adaptation of a light impressionistic palette. One of twenty-one paintings left by Adelaide Milton de Groot to the American Paintings and Sculpture Department.

John Haberle
1856–1933

A Bachelor's Drawer
  Oil on canvas
  20 x 36 in.
  Signed and dated: .Haberle.1890–1894
  Purchase, Henry R. Luce Gift, 1970.193

Haberle is recognized, along with William Harnett and John Peto, as one of America's most accomplished trompe l'oeil painters. This work, with its extremely shallow space and meticulously rendered details, produces a remarkable illusion of reality and stands as one of the masterpieces of the genre.

Childe Hassam
1859–1935

Avenue of the Allies, 1918
  Oil on canvas
  36 x 28¼ in.
  Signed and dated: Childe Hassam 1918;
    C. H./1918
  Bequest of Miss Adelaide Milton de Groot
    (1876–1967), 67.187.127

Hassam, one of the leading exponents of American impressionism, painted a series of brilliant canvases depicting New York City patriotically bedecked with the flags of the allied nations of World War I. In these fragments of city life he orchestrated waving flags, architecture, and crowds into a single pictorial design.

Harriet Goodhue Hosmer
1830–1908

Daphne
  Marble
  H. 27½ in.
  Signed and inscribed: HARRIET HOSMER/FECIT.
    ROMAE
  Morris K. Jesup Fund, 1973.133

Done about 1854, this sensual bust is one of the sculptor's earliest and finest works. Although a leading neoclassicist, she was not represented in the Museum's rich nineteenth-century American sculpture collection until this piece was purchased.

John Quincy Adams Ward
1830–1910

The Indian Hunter
   Bronze
   H. 16 in.
   Signed and dated: J. Q. A. Ward/1860
   Morris K. Jesup Fund, 1973.257

Ward, trained in America rather than abroad, was one of the leading American sculptors of the second half of the nineteenth century. This statuette, dated 1860, was modeled from life sketches made in the Dakotas, and its success marked the beginning of a half-century in which naturalism dominated American sculpture.

Edward Kemeys
1843–1907

Still Hunt
   Bronze
   22½ x 27 15/16 in.
   Signed: Kemeys (monogramed wolf's head)
   Founder's mark: COPYRIGHT 1894/WINSLOW BROS. CO.
   Rogers Fund, 1972.54

In 1894 Kemeys, America's first successful animalier, produced a series of unique bas-reliefs of the American panther: Feeding, At Bay, Still Hunt, and At Play. This one, the only surviving example of the series, is not an anatomical study but a sensitive, knowledgeable rendering of the feline with all its tension and power suggested.

Henry Merwin Shrady
1871–1922

George Washington at Valley Forge
   Bronze
   H. 25½ in.
   Signed: H. M. SHRADY
   Founder's mark: ROMAN BRONZE N.Y.
   Purchase, Rogers Fund and Charles and Anita Blatt Gift, 1974.9

This is a cast of the final model for the equestrian statue in the Brooklyn Plaza at the Williamsburg Bridge. The heavily draped figure and the wind-blown horse produce a work of enormous mass, evoking a somber, moving portrait of the general at the bleakest and most courageous moment of his career.

Daniel Chester French
1850–1931

Study for a Head
Bronze
H. 17⅝ in.
Signed and dated: Daniel C. French Sc.; DCF/
Oct. 1907
Founder's mark: Jno. WILLIAMS INC./BRONZE
FOUNDRY NY
Purchase, Erving Wolf Foundation Gift, 1974.
324

French was one of America's most talented
Beaux-Arts sculptors and its most prolific sculptor of public monuments. This bust is a study for
the head of the mourning Victory in the Melvin
Memorial, a beautiful and innovative funerary
monument in Concord, Massachusetts, to three
brothers killed in the Civil War. A replica of the
memorial is in the Metropolitan's collection.

American Wing

Comments by   Berry B. Tracy, Curator in Charge (BBT), Morrison H. Heckscher, Curator (MHH), Marilyn Johnson Bordes and Frances Gruber, Associate Curators (MJB, FG), and Jean Mailey, Associate Curator, Textile Study Room (JM)

Office of Adler and Sullivan

Staircase from Chicago Stock Exchange Building
   1893–1895
   Cast iron (electroplated in bronze)
   12 x 7½ x 13 ft.
   Purchase, Emily C. Chadbourne Bequest and
     Mr. and Mrs. James Biddle Gift, 1972.50.1

In the series of splendid office buildings designed in partnership with the engineer Dankmar Adler between 1881 and 1895, Sullivan's main concern was the integration of ornament and architecture. The complex, small-scale geometric motifs of his mature decorative style are cast into the various components of this staircase. A pair of stairs, each of four flights and two stories in height, will be installed in the American Wing as functioning staircases adjacent to a selection of smaller samples of Sullivan's other ornamental styles. MHH

Frank Lloyd Wright

Living room from Francis W. Little house
   Wayzata, Minnesota, 1912–1915
   White oak, electroglazed glass
   30 x 50 x 13½ ft.
   Purchase, Emily C. Chadbourne Bequest,
     1972.60.1

In its imaginative spatial effects, visual interplay between interior and exterior, and use of native materials and natural finishes, this typifies the revolutionary "prairie style" of domestic architecture introduced in the Midwest by Wright in the last decade of the nineteenth century. Complete with its original furnishings, and accompanied by drawings and correspondence demonstrating their evolution, the room is a remarkable document of Wright as the total interior architect.
   MHH

Possibly **Peter Blin**

Chest with two drawers
  Wethersfield, Connecticut, 1675–1705
  Oak, pine, cedar, maple
  H. 39⅞ in.
  Gift of Mrs. J. Woodhull Overton, 66.190.1

Decorated with flat carving, paint, and applied moldings and split spindles and bosses, this shows the tulip and leaf motifs and the boldly shaped turnings characteristic of a group of notable seventeenth-century chests and cupboards from the Connecticut River Valley. The carving, well balanced in design, is particularly crisp in execution.   FG

Chest-on-frame
  Eastern Massachusetts, 1680–1700
  Oak, pine, poplar, maple
  H. 35⅝ in.
  Gift of Mrs. J. Woodhull Overton, 69.209

Elaborate turnings, applied moldings that create arched and octagonal panels, and a sunburst design make this the most ornate of the known chests-on-frame. Since it had only a brief popularity, the form is rare.   FG

High chest of drawers
  Massachusetts, about 1710–1720
  Walnut, walnut veneers, pine
  H. 69½ in.
  Gift of Clarence Dillon, 1975.132.1a,b

This very handsome William and Mary piece is the only known example with projecting corners in its elaborate moldings and fluted pilasters on the front and sides, anticipating the Queen Anne style. It belonged to Edward Holyoke, president of Harvard College, 1737–1769. A walnut Queen Anne dressing table, related to the chest through its stop-fluted pilasters, was included in the gift to the Museum.   FG

Chest of drawers
  Newport, about 1750–1760
  Mahogany
  H. 34 in.
  Purchase, Emily C. Chadbourne Bequest and
    Gifts of Mrs. J. Amory Haskell, Mrs. Russell
    Sage, and George Coe Graves (The Sylmaris
    Collection), by exchange, 1972.130

This, the only known eighteenth-century American chest of drawers with marble top and serpentine sides, is the closest American equivalent to the French commode. The serpentine sides and shaped corners, the front feet with sharply carved talons, and the rear pad feet are all typical features of Newport workmanship, specifically that of the cabinetmaker John Goddard.   MHH

Sofa
  Philadelphia, about 1760–1775
  Mahogany
  L. 97¾ in.
  Gift of Mrs. Louis Guerineau Myers in memory
    of her husband, by exchange, 1972.55

This simple, eminently successful sofa has all the features of the classic Philadelphia camelback pattern—boldly serpentined back rail, broadly scrolled arms, and straight Marlborough legs with substantial cuffs.   MHH

Pembroke table
  Philadelphia, 1765–1775
  Mahogany
  H. 28 in.
  Purchase, Emily C. Chadbourne Bequest,
    1974.35

One of the choicest examples of the Philadelphia Chippendale version of the breakfast or Pembroke table. It retains its original finish, much mellowed with age.   MHH

Card table
  Newport, about 1760–1775
  Mahogany
  H. 28 in.
  Friends of the American Wing Fund, 67.114.1

The blocking of the skirts, the upright balls and open talons of the claw and ball feet, and the flat, stylized leaf carving on the knees are all features of Newport cabinetwork, but in perfection of form and precision of execution this example stands out from its peers.   MHH

Easy chair
  Massachusetts, about 1760–1775
  Mahogany
  H. 47½ in.
  Friends of the American Wing Fund, 67.114.2

Faultless proportions and masterly execution make this one of the finest examples of the form. The modern red silk damask has been upholstered in the eighteenth-century manner with gimp-covered piping.   MHH

Chest-on-chest
  Philadelphia, about 1765–1775
  Mahogany
  H. 97½ in.
  Friends of the American Wing Fund, J. Aaron
    & Co. Gift, Virginia Groomes Gift in memory
    of Mary W. Groomes, 1975.91

With its naturalistic phoenix finial as a foil to the severely architectural form of the case below, this epitomizes Philadelphia Chippendale case furniture. A surviving ledger account suggests that the finial may have been carved by the looking-glass-maker James Reynolds, the case piece executed by Thomas Affleck.   MHH

Probably **Benjamin Randolph**

Side chair
  Philadelphia, about 1770
  Mahogany
  H. 36 in.
  Sansbury-Mills and Rogers Funds; Emily C.
    Chadbourne Gift; Virginia Groomes Gift in
    memory of Mary W. Groomes; Mr. and Mrs.
    Marshall P. Blankarn Gift; John Bierwirth
    and Robert G. Goelet Gifts; Gifts of George
    Coe Graves (The Sylmaris Collection), and
    Mrs. Russell Sage, by exchange; and funds
    from various donors, 1974.325

The unique cross-shaped splat, saddle seat, scalloped seat rails, and "hairy paw" feet make this
chair (one of a set of which five others are known)
the richest of all American Chippendale examples. The set was probably made for General
John Cadwalader.   MHH

Candle stand
  Connecticut, 1770–1800
  Cherry
  H. 28½ in.
  Gift of Mrs. Alan W. Carrick, 69.207

American candle stands in the Queen Anne and
Chippendale styles are rare. One of a small group
of pieces from the Norwich, Connecticut, area,
with finely carved Corinthian capital on the
fluted column, and with layered leaf carving on
the knees, this is an ambitious and unusually
successful vernacular interpretation of the Boston
Chippendale style.   MHH

Secretary-bookcase
  Philadelphia, about 1790
  Mahogany veneers over pine, light wood inlays,
    painted decoration
  H. 8 ft. 6½ in.
  Purchase, Joseph Pulitzer Bequest, 67.203

The glazing was altered about 1840. Study of the
scars of the original mullions on the doors, and
comparison with possible choices in cabinetmakers' pattern books of the period, enabled us
to restore the original design.   MJB

John and Thomas Seymour

Sideboard
   Boston, about 1800–1810
   Mahogany
   L. 73 in.
   Gift of the family of Mr. and Mrs. Andrew
      Varick Stout in their memory, 65.188.1

One of two nearly identical sideboards representing the richest casework of the Seymours of Boston and the last example of this quality to be held in a private collection. MJB

Secretary-bookcase
   Salem, Massachusetts, 1800–1810
   Mahogany, satinwood
   H. 8 ft.
   Mrs. Russell Sage Gift, Bequest of Ethel Yocum,
      Bequest of Charlotte C. Hoadley, and Rogers
      Fund, by exchange, 1971.9

One of the most successful of the dozen or so "Salem secretaries" known, this fine Federal piece has an unusually integrated design based largely upon a repetition of surface ovals. MJB

John Geib & Son

Pianoforte
   New York, 1804–1814
   Mahogany
   Gift of Eric M. Wunsch, 69.259

The richly ornamented case reflects all the varieties of cabinet ornament that were typical of the finest New York furniture of the time. Traditionally, Geib's cases were made in the shop of Duncan Phyfe. The actions of most pianofortes of the period were imported, but Geib made his own.
   BBT

Card table
  Baltimore, about 1805
  Painted wood
  H. 29¾ in.
  Purchase, Mrs. Russell Sage Gift, 1970.189

The first example of fine painted Baltimore Federal furniture to enter the Wing, this is attributed to the shop of John and Hugh Findlay. It is related to a similar and documented set owned by the Baltimore Museum of Art.   MJB

Bookcase desk
  Baltimore or Philadelphia, about 1811
  Mahogany, satinwood, églomisé
  H. 91 in.
  Purchase, Gifts of Mrs. Russell Sage and various other donors, 69.203

The design is based on the "Sisters' Cylinder Bookcase" in Thomas Sheraton's *Cabinet Dictionary* (1803). A pencil inscription on one drawer reads "M Oliver Married the 5 of October 1811 Baltimore."   MJB

Curtis and Dunning

Banjo clock
  Concord, Massachusetts, about 1815
  Carved and gilded wood
  Bequest of Flora E. Whiting, 1971.180.36

From the bequest of one of America's most prodigious collectors comes this pristine example with original parcel gilding and églomisé tablets in soft yellows and greens.   MJB

Duncan Phyfe

Pair of pier tables
 New York, about 1815
 H. 34 in.
 Gift of John C. Cattus, 67.262.2,3

By 1817 the fashionable drawing rooms of New York town houses were furnished with tables at every pier, the space between the pairs of front and rear windows, or on each side of the chimney breast. These, with their reeded legs and fluted ovolo corners, graced one of the finest Federal houses, that of Moses Rogers at 7 State Street, overlooking the Battery. BBT

Charles-Honoré Lannuier

Sideboard
 New York, about 1815
 Mahogany
 H. 43 in.
 Gift of Fenton L. B. Brown, 1972.235.1

Until this monumental classical piece appeared in 1972, only one other large case piece by the great Parisian émigré Lannuier was known: the wardrobe in the New-York Historical Society. Lannuier worked at 60 Broad Street from 1803 to 1819, making furniture for a wide variety of notables including Stephen Van Rensselaer in Albany and Henri Christophe, the self-styled emperor of Haiti. BBT

Charles-Honoré Lannuier

Card table
 New York, about 1815
 Bird's-eye maple, rosewood veneer
 H. 31 in.
 Purchase, Funds from various donors, 66.170

Of the seven Lannuier figural card tables known, this is one of the richest in exhibiting all the methods of the Frenchman's ornamentation: brass inlaid details of palmettes, circles, and stars as well as an ormulu mount on the top edge and apron, contrast of light bird's-eye maple and dark rosewood veneer with verde antique and parcel gilding. Unique is the playing surface, a circular inset of red baize. MJB

Attributed to John and Hugh Findlay

Four side chairs
  Baltimore, about 1815–1820
  Maple
  H. 34 in.
  Purchase, Mrs. Paul Moore Gift, 65.167.1,3,5,9

One of a set of nine, each with a different design on the tablet, this, in the Empire style of the English Regency, is reminiscent of the suite, for which the Findlays' designs survive, made for the White House during the Madison Administration (1809–1817).   BBT

Pair of girandole looking-glasses
  New York, about 1817
  Carved wood, gilt gesso
  H. about 54 in.
  Gift of Mrs. Frederick Moseley, Jr., 1974.363.1,2

Made for the town house of Stephen Van Rensselaer and his bride, Harriet Elizabeth Bayard, in Albany. The house was designed by Philip Hooker and furnished in the richest fashion by Lannuier and Phyfe, the leading cabinetmakers of New York. The Wing did not previously own such an early pair with facing eagle finials.   BBT

Sofa
  Probably New York, about 1820
  Mahogany, ash, maple, pine
  L. 97⅜ in.
  Friends of the American Wing Fund, 65.58

One of the most stylish examples of its time, this antique Grecian sofa with dolphin feet shows an extraordinary sweep of line and virtuosity of decorative detail.   MJB

Duncan Phyfe

Pair of card tables
  New York, about 1825–1830
  Rosewood
  H. 29½ in.
  Edgar J. Kaufmann Charitable Foundation
    Fund, 68.94.1,2

From the mid-eighteenth century, card tables were made and sold in pairs, but it is a rare thing to find them surviving together like these superb specimens in the late classical taste of the Greek Revival period.   BBT

Counter
  New Lebanon, New York, about 1825–1835
  Pine
  H. 32¾ in.
  Friends of the American Wing Fund, 66.10.14

Its parallel banks of drawers prophetic of modern functional furniture, this was used in a weave-room of the sisters' shop at the New Lebanon Shaker community. It is one of more than forty Shaker-made objects acquired at one time for installation in a Shaker interior in the American Wing.   MHH

Workshop of Duncan Phyfe

Pair of meridiennes
  New York, 1837
  Mahogany
  L. 74 in.
  L. E. Katzenbach Fund Gift, 66.221.1

The style of the French restauration is interpreted in these pieces made for New York lawyer Samuel A. Foot. Of massive grandeur, they are the best expression of a style which, when mass produced, was popularly termed "pillar and scroll."   MJB

Forestville Clock Manufactory

Acorn Clock
    Bristol, Connecticut, about 1849–1853
    Rosewood
    Gift of Mrs. Paul Moore, 1970.289.6

The case is made of laminated rosewood, like Belter furniture of the mid-nineteenth century. The movement is of the rare "wagon spring" variety.   BBT

Joseph Meeks and Sons

Armchair (part of a parlor suite)
    New York, 1850s
    Rosewood
    H. 48 in.
    Gift of Bradford A. Warner, 69.258.4

Not many years ago this laminated rococo revival piece would undoubtedly have been attributed to the New York factory of John Henry Belter; it is, however, documented as a product of his competitors J. and J. W. Meeks and thus serves as a basis of attribution for an entire group of related furniture forms.   MJB

Alexander Roux

Etagère
    New York, 1850–1857
    Rosewood
    Sansbury-Mills Fund, 1971.219

Labeled by the French-born New York cabinet-maker, this is a summit example of the rococo revival style, as well as a valuable complement and contrast to the Wing's pierced and laminated rococo furniture by Roux's competitor John Henry Belter.   MJB

Herter Brothers

Wardrobe
New York, 1880
Cherry, ebonized and inlaid
H. 78½ in.
Gift of Kenneth O. Smith, 69.140

Perhaps the finest example of American art furniture known, this shows the decorative influences of both Japan and England. It was once
owned by Lillian Russell. MJB

Herter Brothers

Library table
New York, about 1882
Rosewood
H. 31¼ in.
Purchase, Mrs. Russell Sage Gift, 1972.47

From the Fifth Avenue home of William H.
Vanderbilt. With its intricate mother-of-pearl and
brass inlay and its finely executed carving, it
represents the best of American furniture in the
Beaux-Arts tradition. MJB

Tobey Furniture Company

Table (part of a dining room suite)
Chicago, about 1890
Cherry
H. 29 9/16 in.
Gift of Mrs. Frank W. McCabe, 68.214.1

Related in its strong lines, massive character, and
decorative carved details to the architectural
works of the Chicago School at the end of the
nineteenth century, this, with its similarity to
works of Louis Sullivan, represents an important
addition to the Wing's collection of late nineteenth-century reform furniture. MJB

Christian Dorflinger, Greenpoint Glass Works

Compote
   Brooklyn, 1861
   Glass, blown, cut, engraved
   H. 7½ in.
   Gift of Mrs. Kathryn Hait Dorflinger Manchee,
      1972.232.1

Elegantly designed, showing the restraint and predilection for engraving and shallow cutting typical of fine glassware of the 1860s, this bears the United States coat of arms on an engraved border of leaves, scrolls, and flowers. From the State Service ordered by Mrs. Lincoln for the White House.   FG

Tiffany Studios

Table lamp
   New York, about 1910
   Bronze and leaded glass
   H. 26½ in.
   Gift of Hugh J. Grant, 1974.214.15a,b

Tiffany was a genius at transmuting plant life into metal and glass. The long-stem lilies of the shade grow out of the exquisitely modeled ten-light lily-pad pedestal and base. With several other lamps in the same gift, the first Tiffany lighting fixtures acquired by the Museum.   MHH

Flowerpot with stand
   Pennsylvania, about 1824
   Glazed earthenware
   H. 9⅞ in.
   Purchase, Virginia Groomes Gift in memory of
      Mary W. Groomes, 1974.7a,b

An exuberant example of folk pottery, this sharply tapering globular pot and its separate stand are edged with a lavishly crimped border. Both are glazed in a warm brown mottled with light yellow and a few splashes of green. The pot is inscribed: Tacy Lewis Newtown Township Delaware County/ 10th Mo./ 5th/ 1824.   FG

Coverlet
>Chinese, for the New England market, 1830s
>Satin, embroidered with plied and floss silks
>115 x 101 in.
>Purchase, Everfast Fabrics, Inc. Gift, 69.241

Flowers, butterflies, and garden scenes were favorite ornaments on the charming silks and porcelains of the China trade, brought back to Salem and Newport by New England's clipper ships in the 1830s, 40s, and 50s. JM

Quilt
>Baltimore, about 1845–1850
>Cotton, printed and unprinted
>96 x 96 in.
>Sansbury-Mills Fund, 1974.24

One of the finest of a group of friendship quilts made in Baltimore, this appears to have been designed and at least partially executed by just one woman, whose imagination and decorative sense place her in the forefront of American quiltmakers of any period. MJB

Quilt
>Ohio, 1870–1880
>Silk and silk velvet
>76½ x 74 in.
>Purchase, Virginia Groomes Gift in memory of
>   Mary W. Groomes, 1974.34

Subtle juxtapositions of color, striking design, and unusually fine quilting make this Amish bridal quilt one of the most unusual known. MJB

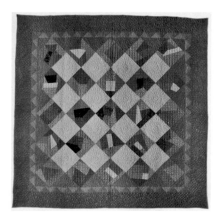

Ancient Near Eastern Art

Comments by   Vaughn E. Crawford, Curator in Charge

Ax head
    Scythian, 6th–5th c. B.C.
    Silver shaft, iron blade
    H. 4 3/16 in.
    H. Dunscombe Colt Fund, 65.4

A curled lion decorates the silver cap, and a pair of falcons project below the iron blade on each side.

Sword
    Sasanian (Iran), 6th–7th c. A.D.
    Gold hilt and scabbard, iron blade
    L. 39½ in.
    Rogers Fund, 65.28

Garnets, glass inlay, and granulation adorn the hilt and front of the scabbard. The front of the scabbard bears an imbricated pattern. The back has a double rib down the center flanked at intervals by five pairs of double spirals.

Head of Sasanian king
Sasanian (Iran), Shapur II (?) (310–379 A.D.)
  Silver
  H. 15⅜ in.
  Fletcher Fund, 65.126

The head is raised from a single piece of silver,
details in repoussé, chased and gilded.

Standard
  Luristan (Iran), about 9th C. B.C.
  Bronze
  H. 6 in.
  Edith Perry Chapman Fund, 66.104.1

Two confronted demons, male and female, with
ibex horns and long ears, stand on a ring and grasp
a second ring.

Bull figurine
  Proto-Elamite (Iran), about 3000 B.C.
  Silver
  H. 6⅜ in.
  Joseph Pulitzer Bequest, 66.173

A bull in human attitude and dress kneels holding
a tall spouted vessel between the hooves of his
forelegs.

Ewer
  Sasanian (Iran), 6th–7th c. a.d.
  Silver-gilt
  H. 13 7/16 in.
  Mr. and Mrs. C. Douglas Dillon Gift and Rogers
    Fund, 67.10a,b

Complete with handle and lid, the body is decorated with four female dancers holding various
objects. Each figure is set in an elaborate arcade.
Inscribed on foot in Pahlavi.

Bowl
  Sasanian (Iran), 3rd–4th c. a.d.
  Silver
  D. 9⅝ in.
  Harris Brisbane Dick Fund, 1970.5

This cast, hemispherical bowl, without base or
interior decoration, bears five busts of the same
female royal personage on its exterior. The higher
relief portions of the busts are applied. Details are
chased.

Plate: a king hunting
  Sasanian (Iran), Yezdegird I (399–421 a.d.)
  Silver-gilt
  D. 9 1/16 in.
  Harris Brisbane Dick Fund, 1970.6

The king spears a stag. The portions of the figure
in relief are applied. Trace of inscription on foot.

Wine bowl
   Sasanian (Iran), 6th–7th c. A.D.
   Silver-gilt
   D. 5 5/16 in.
   Mrs. Constantine Sidamon-Eristoff Gift, 1970.7

The central medallion contains a lion. The six surrounding medallions depict the story of wine making. The interior is undecorated.

Roundel
   Sarmatian (Iran), 3rd–2nd c. B.C.
   Silver covered with gold foil on iron back
   D. 5 3/16 in.
   Purchase, Bequest of Florance Waterbury, 1970.132

A recumbent horned animal lies coiled in the center surrounded by a circle of inlays, another circle consisting of two lions and two griffins, and a second circle of inlays. These are made of turquoise-colored stone or paste.

Male head
   Isin-Larsa (Mesopotamia), about 2000 B.C.
   Terracotta
   H. 7⅛ in.
   Rogers Fund, 1972.96

Traces of red paint appear on the skin and traces of black material on the hair. The coarse orange buff ware is broken at the neck.

Jar
  Sumerian (Mesopotamia), about 2500 B.C.
  Alabaster
  L. 5 1/16 in.
  Gift of Alastair Bradley Martin, 1973.33.1

The two ends depict horned female deities with bovine ears and long plaited hair. One side bears a worn inscription.

Ibex on stand
  Sumerian (Mesopotamia), about 2500 B.C.
  Bronze
  H. 15 11/16 in.
  Rogers Fund, 1974.190

The head was cast separately and pinned into place. The upper stand, with four rings, may have been used to support offering bowls. The lower stand, to which the ibex was fastened by tenons, is similar in form to others from excavations in the Diyala region.

Male head
  Eastern Iran, 5th–8th C. A.D.
  Terracotta
  H. 9 in.
  Purchase, Joseph Pulitzer Bequest, 1974.210

The light reddish brown fabric of this handsomely modeled head is tempered with white and black sand. Broken at the neck, with the impression of a tied reed bundle visible on the interior surface.

Arms and Armor

Comments by   Helmut Nickel, Curator

Court sword
>French, 1775–1785
>Hilt silver-gilt
>L. 39⅝ in.
>Gift of Heribert Seitz, 65.228

Given as a token of esteem for the four-month fellowship in the Museum that enabled the donor to study our collection in preparation for his publication on edged weapons, *Blankwaffen* (Braunschweig, 1965).

Ceremonial sword
>Siamese, 18th c.
>Hilt and scabbard embossed gold
>L. 36¼ in.
>Gift of their Majesties, King Bhumipol Adul-
>   yadej and Queen Sirikit of Thailand, 67.120

This sword was given at a dinner party in the Museum during the exhibition *In the Presence of Kings.*

Chess knight
  English (?), about 1370
  Ivory
  H. 2 3/16 in.
  Pfeiffer Fund, 68.95

The only known sculpture in the round, made
before the sixteenth century, of a knight on a
fully armored horse. It was in English private
collections during the nineteenth century but disappeared from sight around 1900, after plaster
casts of it were made. These served as illustrations for more than two generations. The original was rediscovered in a private collection in
Dublin.

Battle-ax
  Mamluk, about 1400
  Steel with gold damascening
  L. (of blade) 11 in.
  Bashford Dean Fund, 69.156

Bearing the blazon of Nawruz al-Hafizi, Vice-
roy of Syria and Governor of Damascus (1397–
1414), this is the oldest Mamluk battle-ax known,
by about three-quarters of a century. Further-
more, by reason of its owner having been the
Governor of Damascus, it is one of the very few
arms with "damascening" that was actually made
in Damascus. It was bought from a visitor from
New Jersey, after it had turned up in the prover-
bial attic.

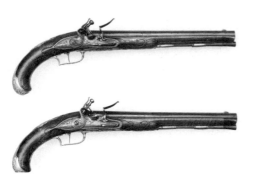

Pair of flintlock pistols
  German (Regensburg), 1760–1780
  by Johann Andreas Kuchenreuter
  L. 17 in.
  Bashford Dean Fund, 69.295.1,2

Our collection of well over one hundred flintlock
pistols of the eighteenth century, consisting
largely of bequests and gifts of private collectors,
lacked a German specimen. This fine pair, by the
most renowned of the Kuchenreuter gunsmith
clan, rounds out the collection.

Rapier
  German/Spanish, 1606
  Signed: Israel Schuech, 1606
  Blade signed: Juan Martinez en Toledo
  Hilt, gilt bronze and jewels
  L. 48 in.
  Fletcher Fund, 1970.77

Made for Christian II, Duke of Saxony and Elector of the Holy Roman Empire, by the court goldsmith Israel Schuech, this was one of the swords that are the glory of the Historische Museum, Dresden, the former Royal Saxon Armory. It is by any standard the finest rapier that has come up for sale during the last thirty years.

Flintlock garniture (hunting rifle, 2 pistols)
  French (Versailles), before 1809
  By Nicolas Noël Boutet
  L. (gun) 45 5/16, (pistols) 17⅛ in.
  Fletcher Fund, 1970.179.la–q

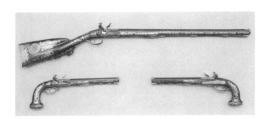

The parade arms made by Boutet as diplomatic presents for Napoleon are among the supreme masterpieces of the gunsmith's art. Our collection had several representative pieces by Boutet, but no full-size pistols. This garniture not only fills this gap, but turned out to be an important clue to the working methods of Boutet's shop. The rifle is signed on the name escutcheon with the owner's name, Nikolai Pompeyevich Chabelsky, and the same name is stamped in the wood of the stock under the silver mountings. This indicates an assembly-line operation where several pieces of identical design, but already assigned different owners, were finished simultaneously.

Two daggers (tanto)
  Japanese, 19th c.

  1) Blade dated 1399
  L. 16½ in.
  Gift of Samuel B. Webb, 1971.251

  2) Blade dated 1330
  L. 15⅞ in.
  Gift of J. Watson Webb, 1972.12

Once part of the Havemeyer Collection, these daggers were given by Mrs. Havemeyer to her grandsons about 1915 and thus did not enter the Museum with the rest of the Havemeyer Collection in 1929.

Helmet crest
> Italian, second half of 16th c.
> Steel, damascened in gold
> H. 7¼ in.
> Gift of Mrs. George Henry Warren in memory
> of her husband, 1972.144.4

Crests of any description are rare, and of sixteenth-century metal crests there are barely half a dozen in existence. This one—a seven-headed hydra, the badge of the family Pallavicini-Sforza—belongs to a helmet and armor garniture most of whose elements are now in the State Hermitage Museum, Leningrad.

Flintlock fowling piece
> French (Lisieux), about 1615
> by Pierre and Marin Le Bourgeoys
> L. 55 in.
> Rogers and Harris Brisbane Dick Funds, 1972.223

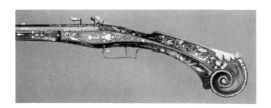

One of the earliest known flintlocks, this bears the mark of Pierre Le Bourgeoys, who together with his brothers Marin and Jean, is credited with the invention of this ignition system. Two other flintlock guns from the Le Bourgeoys workshop survive, one in the Musée de l'Armée, Paris, the other in the State Hermitage Museum, Leningrad. Ours bears the crowned cipher of Louis XIII of France (1601–1643) and the inventory number 134 of his Cabinet d'Armes.

Group of five swords
> Italian, Spanish, German, 15th and 16th c.
> L. 49 3/16, 34½, 47 1/16, 47⅛, 47 5/16 in.
> Bequest of Col. Wickliffe P. Draper, 1973.27.1–5

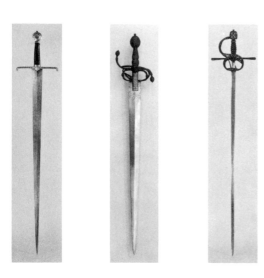

The will of Colonel Draper enabled the Museum to pick five swords from his collection before it was sold at auction. The five are either well-known pieces by makers not represented in our collection or of a special type not yet present. The first is a knightly sword of early fifteenth-century cruciform type, with silver-plated hilt enameled with ivy vines (for the motto "Je meurs où je m'attache"). The second is a rapier with pineapple-patterned hilt, dated 1560 and signed by Daniele da Serravalle (died 1565), who worked for Emperor Charles V and for the dukes of Milan. Its blade is older by at least a generation and bears the mark of one of the celebrated Passau swordsmiths. The third, a rapier with a hilt of intricately cut steel, bears on its blade—pierced

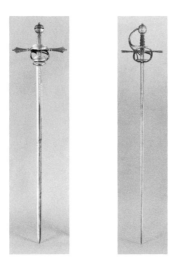

by 660 tiny decorative holes—the signature of the Belluno swordsmith Pietro da Formicano (active about 1600). The fourth is a silver-mounted Saxon *Reitschwert* (late sixteenth century) with globular pommel, one of the four distinctive shapes of these swords that was lacking in our collection. This sword still has its silver-mounted scabbard. The fifth, a rapier with silver-encrusted hilt, bears the stagmark of the bladesmith Mewes Berns, Solingen (active 1610–1615).

Hunting gun
> German, 1705–1710
> Attributed to Herman Bongarde, Düsseldorf,
>   after designs by Lacollombe, published 1702
> L. 56½ in.
> Bashford Dean Fund, James Elwood Jones, Jr.,
>   Gift, and Rogers and Fletcher Funds, 1974.4

In the French tradition of design as introduced into Germany by Herman Bongarde. As a tour de force in cut steel, it is the best example of this technique in the collection.

Target gun (Schuetzenrifle)
> German (Munich), about 1860
> by Carl Stiegele
> L. 43 in.
> Rogers Fund, 1974.10

Probably made as a prize for a marksmen's contest (Schützenfest), this gun, with its exceptionally fine damascus-steel barrel and rich carvings of folkloric scenes, represents the German equivalent of Victorian style at its richest.

The Costume Institute

Comments by   Stella Blum, Curator

Man's sleeved waistcoat
   English, 1747
   L. at center back 33½ in.
   Purchase, Irene Lewisohn Bequest, CI 66.14.2

Of porcelain blue silk with a rich brocading of silver and silver-gilt foliate forms entwined with realistic flowers in polychrome silk on fronts, skirts, pocket flaps, and cuffs, this is an extremely rare example of Spitalfields silk for which the exact design exists. The original pattern for the brocade, drawn by Anna Maria Garthwaite for "Mr. Lekeux" and dated October 23, 1747, is in the Print Department of the Victoria and Albert Museum.

Gown
   English, about 1750–1775
   L. at center back 47¼ in.
   Purchase, Irene Lewisohn Bequest, CI 66.34

An early variation of the English back (corsage en fourreau), this is of white linen embroidered with polychrome silks in a pattern of floral and fruit sprays, small sprigs, and vases of flowers, executed chiefly in satin, stem, and Kensington stitches.

Court dress
   English, about 1760
   L. at center back 49 in.
   Purchase, Irene Lewisohn Bequest, CI
      65.13.1a–c

A formal court gown of bodice, stomacher, and skirt in delphinium blue silk, self-patterned and brocaded in silver thread in a pattern of rosettes interspersed with rose sprays, carnations, and plumes, and trimmed with silver lace, tinsel, and braid passementerie.

Man's coat
   French (?), about 1778–1785
   L. at center back 41½ in.
   Gift of Lilly Daché, CI 68.45

Typical of the rich materials and fine embroidery fashionable at the period, this is of voided velvet— black cut pile on purplish blue ground—with a small allover stylized peacock-feather design in gold. The bold floral and foliate embroidery is executed in multicolored pastel silks.

Gown and matching petticoat
   American, about 1780–1785
   L. at center back (gown) 66, (petticoat) 37½ in.
   Gift of the heirs of Emily Kearny Rogers
      Cowenhoven, 1970.87a,b

Of golden yellow silk handpainted in China with a design of flowers and butterflies, this fashionably short gown has a closed bodice with English back and a skirt with interior ties to be worn *à la Polonaise* over silk paniers. The gown was worn by the second wife of Jonathan Belcher, who had been, seriatim, the governor of Massachusetts, New Hampshire, and Vermont.

Gown and matching petticoat
   French, about 1785
   L. at center back (gown) 60, (petticoat) 37 in.
   Purchase, Irene Lewisohn Bequest, CI 66.39a,b

Of red-lavender and white striped silk taffeta, this very fashionable *robe à l'anglaise* was re-made to its present form from an earlier dress of about 1760, probably a sack dress or a *robe à la française.*

Morning dress
   English, about 1827
   L. at center back 53 in.
   Purchase, Irene Lewisohn Bequest, 1972.139.9

A charming example of the modish printed cotton dresses of the third and fourth decades of the nineteenth century, this is of white muslin printed with a red and green floral stripe against a black-dotted ground forming stylized flowers. The ex-aggerated puffed sleeves are characteristic of the period.

Ball gown
   American, about 1854
   L. at center back (bodice) 14, (skirt) 46½ in.
   Gift of Mary Pierrepont Beckwith, CI 69.14.2

Of ivory silk net over white silk taffeta, the ruffles edged with black lace and accented with bou-quets of pink and white artificial flowers. Mrs. Edwards Pierrepont, who wore this gown and several that follow, was the wife of Judge Ed-wards Pierrepont, Attorney General of the United States in 1875.

Afternoon dress
> American, about 1858
> L. at center back (bodice) 13⅛, (skirt) 47 in.
> Gift of Mary Pierrepont Beckwith, CI 69.14.9a,b

The two-piece dress in tones of gray, light blue, and ivory, is a chiné-flowered taffeta with large-scale check trimmed in bright blue silk ruching edged with black ribbon and blonde lace. Like the preceding gown, it was worn by Mrs. Edwards Pierrepont.

Ball gown
> French (Paris), 1865
> Label: E. Pingat et Cie
> L. at center back (bodice) 13, (skirt) 62¾ in.
> Gift of Mary Pierrepont Beckwith, CI 69.33.12a,b

Of oyster white silk faille trimmed with bands of black lace dotted in gilt, black velvet appliqués, and black chenille fringe, this two-piece gown was made for Mrs. Edwards Pierrepont.

Ball gown
> American, about 1870
> L. at center back (bodice) 13½, (skirt) 65 in.
> Gift of Mary Pierrepont Beckwith, CI 69.14.1a,b

This two-piece gown is of peony pink silk faille trimmed with ruffles of matching silk gauze and white beaded lace. It was made for Mrs. Edwards Pierrepont.

Dinner dress
  French (Paris), 1873
  Label: A. Corbay
  L. at center back (bodice) 22, (skirt) 77 in.
  Gift of Margaret M. Flockhart, CI 68.53.3a,b

This two-piece dress of robin's-egg blue silk faille, trimmed with ruffles of aquamarine net, with fichu and puffed undersleeves of white mousseline, was made by one of the most fashionable Parisian dressmakers of the period. It was worn by Fannie Davis Whitfield, mother of Mrs. Andrew Carnegie.

Reception dress
  French (Paris), about 1878
  Label: Mon Vignon
  L. at center back (bodice) 32, (skirt) 76½ in.
  Gift of Mary Pierrepont Beckwith, CI 69.14.12a,b

Of pale champagne floral-patterned silk and plain cream satin, this dress has the fashionable cuirass basque and trained bustle skirt elaborately trimmed with passementerie of frost white beads, silk and chenille fringe, and dark green silk velvet. It was worn by Mrs. Edwards Pierrepont.

Tailored wedding ensemble and traveling costume
  American (New York), 1887
  Label: H. Rossberg
  L. at center back (bodice-jacket) 20, (skirt) 43 in.
  Gift of Margaret M. Flockhart, CI 68.53.5a–d

Worn by Mrs. Andrew Carnegie (née Louise Whitfield) at her evening wedding on April 22, 1887, and afterward for going away to England, the ensemble includes two jackets of slightly different cut and length, and a bustle skirt with asymmetrical drapery. Of gray worsted wool trimmed with rose-gray passementerie.

Kilt costume
  Scottish, 1888
  L. at center back (bodice-jacket) 15½, (skirt)
    42½ in.
  Gift of Margaret M. Flockhart, CI 68.53.7a,b

Made for Mrs. Andrew Carnegie during her first
summer at Cluny Castle in the Scottish highlands.
The severely tailored jacket is of navy wool
trimmed with black braid, and the pleated bustle
skirt is in the Carnegie tartan (set in navy wool,
deep green and red, overchecked in red and
yellow).

Ball gown
  French (Paris), 1893–1894
  Label: J. Worth
  L. at center back (bodice) 12, (skirt) 48 in.
  Gift of Margaret M. Flockhart, CI 68.53.10a,b

A fine example from a couturier house of first
importance, this is of ivory silk satin sprinkled
with silver sequins and handpainted with a design of blue cornflowers muted by an overlay of
ivory gauze appliqués and accented at neckline
and on sleeves and skirt with pale blue chiffon.
It was made for Mrs. Andrew Carnegie.

Evening dress
  French (Paris), fall 1965
  Label: Balenciaga
  L. shoulder to hem 59 in.
  Gift of Mrs. Charles Wrightsman, CI 66.54.5

A superb example of a design by one of the most
significant couturiers of the twentieth century,
this is of pink point d'esprit patterned net over
matching gazar, with ostrich-feather shafts indi-
vidually applied over the body of the dress. The
sash is of matching satin.

Pair of men's shoes
    European, about 1660–1675
    L. 11½ in.
    Purchase, Irene Lewisohn Bequest, 1973.114.3a,b

Of buff suede with warm brownish red heels and sole edges, an extremely rare survival in the style of the third quarter of the seventeenth century. The red heels continued to be fashionable court wear till the end of the eighteenth century.

Pair of chopines
    Italian (Venice), about 1600
    L. 8¾ in.
    Purchase, Irene Lewisohn Bequest, 1973.114.4a,b

Of white leather decorated with pierced and stamped designs and trimmed with tiny pompoms of silk floss, these are among the very few surviving examples of a fashion almost exclusively Venetian.

Traditional costume: man's coat
    Turkman, 19th c.
    L. at center back 56 in.
    Purchase, Irene Lewisohn Bequest, 1971.38.2

Of purple silk velvet embroidered in a stylized foliate design with silk, gilt, and polychrome silk threads; lining of tie-dyed warp-patterned silk (*ikat*) in golden yellow, deep reddish pink, blue, and pale pink.

Ritual mask headdress
    African (probably BaKuba tribe, Zaïre), early
      20th c.
    H. 18¼ in.
    Gift of Lilly Daché, 1974.83.30

Decorated with cowrie shells and red, white, and
blue glass beads in geometric patterns to form a
facial mask surmounted by a curved bar representing an elephant's truck, this mask is of a type
worn only by men of royal blood. It is used in
initiation rites to symbolize Woot, a cultural hero,
the originator of the political structure, royalty,
and most arts and crafts.

Drawings

Comments by   Jacob Bean, Curator

Lambert Doomer
   1622/23–1700, Dutch

View of Nantes
   Pen and brown ink, gray wash
   9¼ x 14 7/16 in.
   Rogers Fund, 65.48

Doomer was a Rembrandt pupil who, in 1646, made a trip along the Loire River in France. His visual impressions are recorded in a series of sensitive watercolor views of which this is a characteristic example.

Charles-Joseph Natoire
   1700–1777, French

Gardens of the Villa d'Este at Tivoli
   Pen and brown ink, watercolor
   12 5/16 x 18 11/16 in.
   Rogers Fund, 65.65

Natoire, who was long resident in Rome as director of the French Academy, drew many such luminous views of Rome and its environs. This one is dated 1760.

Pesellino (Francesco di Stefano)
1422–1457, Italian

Saint Philip Seated
Brush and brown wash
10¾ x 7½ in.
Rogers Fund, 65.112.1

A rare, recently rediscovered example of the refined draughtsmanship of this Florentine painter who sometimes worked in collaboration with Fra Filippo Lippi.

Peter Paul Rubens
1577–1640, Flemish

Study of a standing female saint
Brush and light brown wash
18⅜ x 12 3/16 in.
Rogers Fund, 65.175

This noble drawing, datable very early in Rubens's career, about 1606–1607, is probably a study for Saint Domitilla in Rubens's altarpiece for the church of Santa Maria in Vallicella, Rome.

Auguste Renoir
1841–1919, French

Sheet of landscape studies
Watercolor
12 x 18½ in.
Rogers Fund, 66.96

This brilliantly colored sheet dates from about 1885.

Carlo Maratti
　1625–1713, Italian

Figure of Divine Wisdom
　Red chalk
　17⅝ x 14 7/16 in.
　Rogers Fund, 66.137

Study for an allegorical figure of Divine Wisdom intended for a section of the frescoed decoration of the great hall of the Palazzo Altieri in Rome.

John Robert Cozens
　1752–1797, English

View of the Villa Lante on the Janiculum in Rome
　Watercolor
　10 x 14½ in.
　Rogers Fund, 67.68

This grandly composed view was drawn during Cozens's second journey to Italy in 1782 when he accompanied the rich and eccentric William Bedford. The villa was designed by the painter and architect Giulio Romano in the early 1520s; in the early nineteenth century it underwent severe modifications.

Paul Gauguin
　1848–1903, French

Tahitian Girl
　Pastel
　15⅜ x 11⅞ in.
　Bequest of Miss Adelaide Milton de Groot
　　(1876–1967), 67.187.13

An exceptionally fine pastel dating from 1892, during Gauguin's first stay in Tahiti.

Georges Seurat
1859–1891, French

Monkey
Conté crayon
12 15/16 x 9 5/16 in.
Bequest of Miss Adelaide Milton de Groot
(1876–1967), 67.187.35

A study for the monkey on a leash that appears in the foreground of Seurat's masterwork, *Sunday on the Island of the Grande Jatte,* a painting of 1885 now in the Art Institute of Chicago.

Jacob Jordaens
1593–1678, Flemish

The Presentation of Jesus in the Temple
Watercolor and gouache
8⅞ x 6¼ in.
Purchase, Florence and Carl Selden Foundation, Inc. Gift, 67.257

Very probably a design for a tapestry; the elaborate architectural framework is characteristic of Jordaens's designs for narrative tapestry series.

Taddeo Zuccaro
1529–1566, Italian

Nude male figure
Red chalk
16⅜ x 11 5/16 in.
Rogers Fund, 68.113

This powerful study was no doubt made in preparation for a figure in a classical procession, probably painted in fresco as an exterior façade design, a speciality of Taddeo Zuccaro's.

Giovanni Paolo Pannini
1691/92–1765, Italian

The Piazza di Montecitorio, Rome
Watercolor
13½ x 21 7/16 in.
Rogers Fund, 68.53

The drawing of the Papal lottery is taking place on the balcony of the Palazzo di Montecitorio, designed by Bernini, finished by Carlo Fontana. On the right is the base of the column of Antoninus Pius, removed later in the eighteenth century to the Vatican and replaced by the obelisk that today dominates the square. This elaborate view was used as the model for a painting by Pannini in the Colville Collection, London.

Salvator Rosa
1615–1673, Italian

Figures around a globe
Pen and brown ink, brown wash, over black chalk
9¼ x 7 13/16 in.
Rogers Fund, 68.56

Rosa was fond of elaborate, enigmatic, allegorical representations. The sense of this group is not clear, though the Italian inscriptions say of one of the figures "he flays," and of another "I scratch."

Giuseppe Ribera
1588/90–1652/56, Spanish

Adoration of the Shepherds
Pen and brown ink, brown wash
9¼ x 7 5/16 in.
Rogers Fund, 68.64

A characteristic example of Ribera's idiosyncratic draughtsmanship, discovered at an auction sale in New York under an incorrect attribution to a sixteenth-century Italian artist.

Guercino (Giovanni Francesco Barbieri)
    1591–1666, Italian

Sleeping Endymion
    Pen and brown ink, brown wash
    8 5/16 x 9¾ in.
    Rogers Fund, 68.171

This nude youth is a study for a sleeping Endymion, probably the one painted in 1650 for Don Antonio Ruffo of Messina and now lost. It was Ruffo who commissioned from Rembrandt the Museum's *Aristotle with the Bust of Homer.*

Raffaellino del Garbo
    About 1466–1524, Italian

Madonna and Child with Attendant Angels
    Pen and brown ink, brown wash
    6⅞ x 8 13/16 in.
    Rogers Fund, 68.204

A fine example of the artist's elegant penmanship, showing his stylistic affinities with Filippino Lippi.

Nicolas de Largillière
    1656–1746, French

Two nude male figures struggling together
    Black and white chalk
    16 11/16 x 21 13/16 in.
    Rogers Fund, 69.10

This powerful academic study was made by Largillière not in his student days but at his full maturity when he was professor at the French Royal Academy of Painting. It was part of a group of figure studies intended to serve as models for his students.

Pierre-Alexandre Wille
1748–1821, French

Two Ladies Making Music in an Interior
Pen and brown ink, colored washes
9 11/16 x 7⅞ in.
Rogers Fund, 69.49

Wille, an artist of German extraction, was one of the most charming "little masters" of late eighteenth-century France. He specialized in scenes like this. The fittings are typical of the Louis XVI style, about 1771, the date of the drawing.

Eugène Delacroix
1798–1863, French

Imaginary portrait of Mathurin Régnier
Watercolor
10½ x 7¼ in.
Rogers Fund, 69.180

This portrait of the late sixteenth-century poet is one of four illustrations Delacroix supplied for the second edition of *Le Plutarque français,* a popular publication extolling the virtues of French worthies of the past.

Annibale Carracci
1560–1609, Italian

Triton Sounding a Conch Shell
Black chalk on blue paper
15¼ x 9½ in.
Rogers Fund, 1970.15

A recently rediscovered study for the triton that appears in the representation of *Thetis Borne to the Wedding Chamber of Peleus* on the ceiling of the gallery of the Palazzo Farnese in Rome, where work on the frescoed decorations began in 1597. The cartoons and the finished fresco are the work of Annibale Carracci's less talented elder brother, Agostino, but the invention of this robustly baroque figure is Annibale's, whose hand is here recognizable, as it is in a further study for the triton in the John Winter collection, London.

Jean-Baptiste Oudry
  1686–1755, French

Angry Swan
  Black and white chalk on blue paper
  9¾ x 15 in.
  Mr. and Mrs. Henry Ittleson, Jr., Fund, 1970.133

Oudry made a specialty of the representation of animals. This study represents a swan attacked by dogs. Other versions exist, one in the North Carolina Museum of Art at Raleigh.

Giovanni Paolo Pannini
  1691/92–1765, Italian

Scalinata della Trinità dei Monti, Rome
  Watercolor
  13 11/16 x 11 9/16 in.
  Rogers Fund, 1971.63.1

A luminous view of the eighteenth-century *scalinata* that meanders from the Piazza di Spagna up to the church of the Trinità dei Monti. No large-scale painting by Pannini of this subject has survived, but he included representations of it in one of his crowded views of the interior of a picture gallery.

Pietro Testa
  1612–1650, Italian

Presentation of the Virgin in the Temple
  Pen and brown ink, brown wash
  14 9/16 x 10 7/16 in.
  Rogers Fund, 1971.241

Study for Testa's most important altarpiece, painted for the church of Santa Croce dei Lucchesi, Rome, and now in the Hermitage, Leningrad.

Annibale Carracci
1560–1609, Italian

Domestic Scene
Pen and black ink, gray wash
12⅞ x 9¼ in.
Purchase, Mrs. Vincent Astor and Mrs. Charles Payson Gifts and Harris Brisbane Dick and Rogers Funds, 1972.133.2

One of the most enchanting of Annibale's observations of domestic life, with a mother warming her child's nightdress before a fire. This probably dates from the early 1580s.

Annibale Carracci
1560–1609, Italian

Two studies of a boy and two of a girl
Red chalk, heightened with white
8⅞ x 12 9/16 in.
Harris Brisbane Dick and Rogers Funds, 1972.133.3

The directness of Annibale's vision and the economy of his use of chalk give to this marvelously beautiful sheet a strikingly modern air. Though the drawing must date from the late 1580s, the incisive notations in rich red chalk anticipate in a prophetic manner the work of Watteau as a draughtsman.

Annibale Carracci
1560–1609, Italian

The Drunken Silenus
Pen and brown ink, brown wash
D. 10 1/16 in.
Harris Brisbane Dick and Rogers Funds, 1972.133.4

Finished design for a silver plaque engraved by Annibale himself for his patron Cardinal Odorado Farnese and intended to be used to decorate the bowl of a standing silver dish, the Tazza Farnese. The plaque, which survives in the Museo Nazionale, Naples, was used for printmaking and pulls from it were taken from a fairly early date.

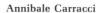

Charles-Antoine Coypel
1694–1752, French

River god and another male figure
    Black chalk
    14 7/16 x 10¾ in.
    Fletcher Fund, 1972.224.2

The god, holding a paddle in his right hand, his left raised in a gesture of defiance, is studied for the figure of Scamandros that appears at the lower left in Coypel's painting of 1737, *Achilles Pursuing the Trojans into the River Scamandros,* now in the Hermitage, Leningrad. The figure at the lower left is a study for one of the drowning Trojans. The connection between this exceptionally vigorous drawing and the Hermitage picture was first noted by Antoine Schnapper.

Jean-Baptiste Greuze
1725–1805, French

Domestic Scene
    Pen and brown ink, gray wash
    13 x 20 in.
    Harris Brisbane Dick Fund, 1972.224.3

A brilliant large-scale example of Greuze's draughtsmanship at its freest and most animated. The scene must represent one of those moralizing themes concerning middle- and working-class life that brought him his great contemporary success.

Eustache Le Sueur
1617–1655, French

Standing male figure with arms and hands bound
    Black and white chalk on gray-washed paper
    16 3/16 x 10 5/16 in.
    Rogers Fund, 1972.224.5

A study for the figure of Saint Gervase used by Le Sueur in a vast tapestry cartoon, now in the Musée du Louvre, representing the Lombard martyrs Saint Gervase and Saint Protase refusing to sacrifice to Jupiter; this was the first of a series of cartoons representing the story of Gervase and Protase, commissioned in 1651 for the Church of Saint Gervais in Paris. Le Sueur designed two of the cartoons; four were supplied after his death by Sébastien Bourdon and Philippe de Champaigne.

Gian Lorenzo Bernini
1598–1680, Italian

Study of a Triton
Red Chalk
14⅜ x 9⅝ in.
Harry G. Sperling Fund, 1973.265

A recently rediscovered drawing in Bernini's own hand for the figure of a triton blowing water from a conch shell. The sea deity rides astride two great shells on the Fontana del Tritone in the middle of the Piazza Barberini, Rome. This vivid sketch is the only example of Bernini's drawn preparation for this splendid and characteristic work of sculpture, datable 1642–1643, that seems to have survived; a pen and wash design at Windsor for the whole fountain scheme appears to be a studio production.

Paolo Veronese
1528–1588, Italian

Sheet of studies for the Allegories of Love
Pen and brown ink, brown wash
12¾ x 8¾ in.
Harry G. Sperling Fund, 1975.150

These brilliant free sketches are Veronese's first ideas for the figure groupings in the four Allegories of Love, paintings probably commissioned by Emperor Rudolph II and now in the National Gallery, London. This drawing, recently rediscovered in a private collection in America, is the only surviving study by Veronese for these celebrated paintings.

Egyptian Art

Comments by   Christine Lilyquist, Curator

Temple and gateway
   Early Roman period (late 1st c. B.C.); from Den-
      dur
   Aeolian sandstone
   L. of gateway and temple about 24.99 m.
   Gift of the Government and People of the Arab
      Republic of Egypt to the Government and
      People of the United States; awarded to the
      Museum by a presidential commission, 68.154

A temple of Egyptian form built by Augustus to
honor two deified brothers.

Statue of Karo
   XIX Dynasty (1320–1200 B.C.)
   Wood
   H. 48 cm.
   Rogers Fund, 65.114

This "Great Craftsman in the Place of Truth" had
tomb number 330 at Deir el Medina.

Seated statue of Siamun
  XVII Dynasty (about 1650–1567 B.C.)
  Limestone
  H. 53.7 cm.
  Rogers Fund, 65.115

Sculpture of this period is rare; this shows a private official in traditional manner.

Statue of a private person
  Early Roman Period (about 30 B.C.)
  Black granite and white stone
  H. 1.17 m.
  Rogers Fund, 65.119

Draped figures wearing rosette circlets seem to have funerary significance.

L-shaped stela from a private tomb
  Late Middle Kingdom (between 1800 and 1700
    B.C.)
  Limestone
  H. 30.5 cm.
  Rogers Fund, 65.120.1,2

The deceased, Sehetepibra, is seated at a table heaped with offerings.

Head of an unknown official
    Reign of Amenhotep III (1417–1379 B.C.)
    Black granite
    H. 12.5 cm.
    Fletcher Fund and the Guide Foundation, Inc.,
      Gift, 66.99.27

A strong private portrait, dated stylistically.

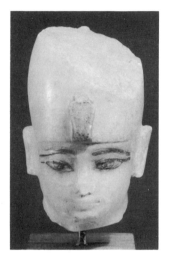

Head of Amenhotep III
    Reign of Amenhotep III (1417–1379 B.C.); found
      by the French expedition of 1798 in the royal
      tomb
    Alabaster
    H. 11.2 cm.
    Fletcher Fund and The Guide Foundation, Inc.,
      Gift, 66.99.29

The king wears the white crown of Upper Egypt.

Head of Amenhotep III
    Reign of Amenhotep III (1417–1379 B.C.)
    Black stone
    H. 9 cm.
    Fletcher Fund and The Guide Foundation, Inc.,
      Gift, 66.99.30

A small portrait of the young king, dated stylistically.

Head of an honored official
   Reign of Amenhotep III (1417–1379 B.C.)
   Hard green stone
   H. 10 cm.
   Fletcher Fund and The Guide Foundation, Inc.,
      Gift, 66.99.31

One of the most appealing small private representations of this splendid era. The owner wears
"collars of gold," or rewards of distinction from
the king.

Sculptor's study
   XVIII Dynasty, reign of Akhenaten (1379–1362
      B.C.); from Amarna, Petrie excavations of
      1891/1892 for Lord Amherst
   Limestone
   H. 34 cm.
   Fletcher Fund and The Guide Foundation Inc.,
      Gift, 66.99.40

A portrait of Akhenaten carved in the severe
style.

Ancestral bust of a private person
   XIX Dynasty (1320–1200 B.C.)
   Painted limestone
   H. 41.2 cm.
   Fletcher Fund and The Guide Foundation, Inc.,
      Gift, 66.99.45

The finest example of this unusual type of Egyptian sculpture.

Block statue of Iuitef/Tjekred
   Third Intermediate Period (about 1085–712
      B.C.); from the Karnak Cachette
   Hard white limestone
   H. 34.3 cm.
   Fletcher Fund and The Guide Foundation, Inc.,
      Gift, 66.99.63

The owner is shown on the front, presenting an offering to Thoth.

Head of a crown prince or priest of Ptah
   XXV Dynasty (about 745–655 B.C.)
   Black granite
   H. 21.8 cm.
   Fletcher Fund and The Guide Foundation, Inc.,
      Gift, 66.99.64

The sidelock on the wig could identify the figure as either subject.

Statuette of a cloaked man
   Mid-XII Dynasty (about 1880 B.C.)
   Hard yellow limestone
   H. 26.6 cm.
   Gift of J. Lionberger Davis, 66.123.1

The pose and the style date this private statue; uninscribed.

Stela made for Ptahmose
  XIX Dynasty (1320–1200 B.C.)
  Limestone
  H. 1.42 cm.
  Harris Brisbane Dick Fund, 67.3

The official Ptahmose is shown adoring Osiris; the inscription contains a hymn to the latter.

Stela of Wenenku
  XIX Dynasty (1320–1200 B.C.)
  Limestone
  H. 45 cm.
  Purchase, J. Lionberger Davis Gift, 67.103

The sun god, Ra Horakhty, sails in his barque above while the owner and his son kneel in adoration below.

False door niche from a tomb
  V Dynasty (about 2494–2345 B.C.)
  Limestone
  W. 75 cm.
  Purchase, Dr. and Mrs. Edmundo Lassalle Gift, 68.13

The owner, whose name means "Beloved of Khufu," is shown with his wife and children.

Relief fragment
  VI Dynasty (about 2345–2181 B.C.)
  Limestone
  W. 38.3 cm.
  Purchase, Lila Acheson Wallace Fund, Inc.,
    Gift, 69.34

Part of a winnowing scene from a private mastaba; traces of paint.

Statue of Anubis
  Ptolemaic Period (323–30 B.C.); from North Saqqara, EES excavations
  Limestone
  L. 64 cm.
  Gift of the Egypt Exploration Society, 69.105

Anubis, shown as he would be posed in watching over a necropolis, is from a Late Period cemetery. Part of the neck is restored.

Statue of Thoth as a baboon
  Ptolemaic Period (323–30 B.C.); from North Saqqara, EES excavations
  Limestone
  H. 69 cm.
  Gift of The Egypt Exploration Society, 1971.51

Impressive sculptural representation. Nose restored.

Statuette of Isis with Horus
  About 650 B.C.?
  Bronze
  H. 20.6 cm.
  Rogers Fund, 1972.62

Isis, the mother of Horus, here wears the horns and disc of Hathor, a cobra circlet, and a vulture headdress.

Statuette of kneeling king
  XXX Dynasty (380–342 B.C.)
  Bronze
  H. 17 cm.
  Bequest of Walter C. Baker, 1972.118.36

The figure, uninscribed, is shown presenting a (missing) offering to a god.

Sphinx of Amenhotep III
  Reign of Amenhotep III (1417–1379 B.C.)
  Faience
  L. 25 cm.
  Purchase, Lila Acheson Wallace Fund, Inc., Gift, 1972.125

An object unique in quality and preservation; fine blue glaze.

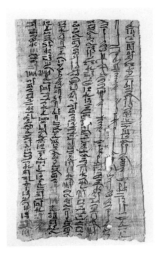

Private letters and accounts
  Late XI–early XII Dynasty (between 2004 and
    1970 B.C.); from Thebes, Museum excavations
  Papyrus
  Largest example 48 x 26.5 cm.
  Rogers Fund, 22.3.516–528

The so-called Hekanakht Papyri with related
documents from the areas of Meketra's and
Harhotep's tombs; accessioned now that study is
completed.

Foundation bricks
  Reign of Ramesses II (1304–1237 B.C.)
  Faience
  L. 26 cm.
  Fletcher Fund and The Guide Foundation, Inc.,
    Gift, 66.99.56–114

The nomen and prenomen of Ramesses II appear
in black on the turquoise green glaze.

Plate
  Early I Dynasty (about 3000 B.C.)
  Schist
  D. 39 cm.
  Purchase, Dr. and Mrs. Edmundo Lassalle Gift,
    68.15

Made for ceremonies at the "Lake of the Building
[called] 'The Stridings of the Gods'" at Memphis.

Sarcophagus
XXI–XXIV Dynasty? (about 1085–712 B.C.); said
to have been found in the Fayuum
Hard white limestone
L. 1.93 m.
Gift of Fanaollah Sobhani, 68.23

The exterior is carved with minor divinities of the
netherworld.

Chair of Renyseneb
Mid-XVIII Dynasty (about 1450 B.C.)
Ebony and ivory
H. 86.2 cm.
Purchase, Patricia R. Lassalle Gift, 68.58

The owner is represented on the slanted back,
seated in a chair of the same type. The seat is
restored according to the original pattern of
matting.

Treasure of diadem, necklaces, earrings,
rings, seals
Late XII–XVII Dynasty (between 1800 and 1567
B.C.); from Es Saliyeh (?)
Gold, crystal, carnelian, lapis lazuli, amethyst,
sard, steatite, faience;
Purchase, Lila Acheson Wallace Fund, Inc.,
Gift, 68.136.1–28

The treasure has Egyptian and Asiatic motifs,
styles, and signs of workmanship.

Mirror
   Mid-XVIII Dynasty (about 1425 B.C.)
   Bronze
   H. 29 cm.
   Bequest of Walter C. Baker, 1972.118.30

The handle is typical of the second half of XVIII
Dynasty. Both the craftsmanship and the completeness of the object make it exceptional.

European Paintings

Comments by   Anthony M. Clark, former Chairman of the Department

Francesco Botticini
About 1446–d. 1497, Italian (Florentine)

Madonna Enthroned
Tempera on wood
110½ x 69 in.
Gift of George Hann, 61.235

This artist's solid, careful technique owes much to Andrea del Castagno, whose influence can be seen here in Botticini's painting of Saints Benedict, Francis, Sylvester, and Anthony Abbot. He also often shows elements borrowed from Botticelli (the angels), Pollaiuolo (the throne), and Verrocchio (the Child). This splendid altar was apparently painted for Ss. Annunziata, Florence, about 1485.

Francisco de Goya y Lucientes
1746–1828, Spanish

Jose Costa y Bonnells, called Pepito
Oil on canvas
41⅜ x 33¼ in.
Gift of Mme. Umberto de Martini, 61.259

The pensive boy was the grandson of the Duke of Alba's doctor and the son of the king of Spain's doctor, important people employed by Goya's chief patrons. Painted about 1813, the child is shown with his wooden horse and his toy drum. The expensive and beautiful clothes are faintly military; the pose is worthy of the conquering Napoleon, although the play is that of an innocent child.

Vincent Van Gogh
1853–1890, Dutch

Oleanders
Oil on canvas
23¾ x 29 in.
Gift of Mr. and Mrs. John L. Loeb, 62.24

This magnificent floral piece, bristling with energy, was painted in Arles in August and September 1888, before the blooming season was over. Oleander bushes Van Gogh described to his brother as "raving mad." The book is Zola's *La Joie de Vivre*.

Philips Koninck
1619–1688, Dutch

Wide River Landscape
Oil on canvas
16¾ x 23½ in.
Anonymous Gift, 63.43.2

A relatively early work by the great panorama painter. Inspired by the somber color and high drama of Rembrandt's landscapes, this painting was long lost and known only through five copies after it.

Gustave Doré
1832–1883, French

The Murder Of Riccio
Oil on canvas
102 x 123¼ in.
Gift of Mr. and Mrs. Sidney C. Norris, 64.226

Doré reputedly painted this scene of British history (Darnley restraining his wife, Mary Queen of Scots, as her secretary is murdered) in England in 1885, and it was refused in that year's Salon, to the dismay of Theophile Gautier. Rembrandt and Veronese are the odd pair of ingredients in the artist's expressive style.

Lorenzo Monaco
1370–1425, Italian (Florentine)

Abraham
Noah
Moses
David

Tempera on wood, gold ground
26 x 17½, 26½ x 17½, 24¾ x 17¾, 22¼ x 17 in.
Purchase, Gwynne M. Andrews Fund, Henry G. Marquand Fund, Bequest of Mable Choate in memory of her father, Joseph Hodges Choat, Gifts of Mrs. Ralph J. Hines, Paul Peralta Ramos, and G. Louise Robinson, 65.14.1–4

In the first decade of the fifteenth century, the exquisite conservative from Siena painted this set of biblical figures. They are shown seated on marble benches placed on colored marble floors, against the gold ground of eternity, holding their symbols. The four were probably arranged in two ranks around a subject of the Christian Salvation which they, as Old Testament heroes, prefigure.

Alfred Sisley
1839–1899, English

The Bridge at Villeneuve-la-Garenne
Oil on canvas
19½ x 25¾ in.
Gift of Mr. and Mrs. Henry Ittleson, Jr., 64.287

An early Sisley, showing the exacting quality, strong observation, and spontaneity of the artist's best work. It belonged to his friend the singer Faure.

Jacques Louis David
1748–1825, French

General Etienne Maurice Gérard,
Marshal of France
Oil on canvas
77⅜ x 32 in.
Rogers and Fletcher Funds and Bequest of Mary Wetmore Shively in memory of her husband, Henry L. Shively, M.D., 65.14.5

Gérard was a hero of rearguard action in the retreat from Russia, and Napoleon made him a peer of France for his actions during the Hundred Days. Both Gérard and David were in exile at Brussels in 1816.

Claude Monet
1840–1926, French

The Customs Watch at Varengeville
Oil on canvas
25¾ x 32 in.
Gift of Mr. and Mrs. Richard Rodgers, 65.21

This is one of Monet's later (1896 or 1897) views of the hut for customs officials at Varengeville. Another view, the McVeigh picture, painted in 1882, is in the Metropolitan's collection.

Lorenzo Lotto
About 1480–1556, Italian (Venetian)

Fra Gregorio Belo of Vicenza
Oil on canvas
34⅝ x 28 in.
Rogers Fund, 65.117

The deeply and complicatedly perceptive, lonely, and lovely vision of Lotto presents a monk holding the homilies of St. Gregory. As a member of the poor hermits of Saint Jerome, the fifty-five-year-old Brother Gregory penitentially beats his chest in the wilderness, remembering that Saint. (The presence of the Crucifixion also recalls Jerome.) Ordered December 9, 1546, this picture was paid for October 11, 1547.

Salvator Rosa
1651–1673, Italian (Neapolitan)

The Dream of Aeneas
Oil on canvas
77½ x 47½ in.
Rogers Fund, 65.118

Virgil (*Aeneid,* VIII, 26 ff.) tells the story of Aeneas, asleep beside the Tiber, seeing in a dream the god of that river who foretells his conquest of Latium. Salvator presents the story powerfully, simply, and with his realistic evocation of nature.

Antonio Alberti
1390–before 1499, Italian (Ferrarese)

Madonna and Child with Pietro di Lardi as Donor, Presented by St. Nicolas
Tempera on wood
43½ x 42 in.
Bequest of Adele L. Lehman in memory of Arthur Lehman, 65.181.5

The verse inscription names the young donor, a prominent Ferrarese noble and official whose coats of arms appear in the lower corners. Although the inscription calls the bishop who introduces Lardi to the Madonna and Child Saint Nicholas, he may be the patron of Ferrara, St. Maurelius. A big painting for Ferrarese art of the first quarter of the fifteenth century, this votive panel comes from the Abbey of Pomposa just outside Ferrara.

Francesco Guardi
1712–1793, Italian (Venetian)

Venice from the Sea
Oil on canvas
48 x 60 in.
Bequest of Adele L. Lehman in memory of
Arthur Lehman, 65.181.8

There is a very large, rather different version of
this picture at Waddesdon (probably Guardi's
largest view), and smaller versions exist, usually
less violent and with fewer gondolas. This one
was painted after 1755, when the Piazza S. Marco
clock grew its third story and probably in the
early 1760s when other topographical details fell
into place.

Claude Lorrain
1600–1682, French

Pastoral Landscape—The Roman Campagna
Oil on canvas
40 x 60 in.
Bequest of Adele L. Lehman in memory of
Arthur Lehman, 65.181.12

The artist painted this imaginary view of an
upper Tiber valley farmhouse in Rome about
1639, listing it in his *Liber Veritatis* as "faict pour
Paris." It is so delicate, open, and atmospheric
that it reminds one of late Corot.

Francesco Francia
About 1450–1517, Italian (Bolognese)

St. Roch
Tempera on wood
85¼ x 59⅜ in.
Gift of George R. Hann, 65.220.1

From the church of S. Maria della Morte, Bologna, this life-size altarpiece was proudly signed
and dated (1502) by the Bolognese artist at the
peak of his career. Venice and Umbria are ingredients of his delicate and noble style.

Giovanni Battista Tiepolo
1696–1779, Italian (Venetian)

The Triumph of Marius
The Capture of Carthage
The Battle of Vercellae
Oil on canvas
127¾ x 124¾, 169½ x 148¼, 170 x 148 in.
Rogers Fund, 65.183.1–3

These large scenes from Roman history were
made for the main hall of Ca' Dolfin in Venice,
the seat of the Patriarch of Aquileia, one of Tiepolo's earliest patrons. There are ten scenes in all;
the rest are at Vienna (2) and Leningrad (5). The
Marius contains Tiepolo's self-portrait—at left
looking at us—and is dated 1729; all were done
by 1732.

Francisco de Zurbaran
1598–1664, Spanish

The Crucifixion
  Oil on canvas
  116¼ x 76½ in.
  Gift of George R. Hann, 65.220.2

The picture is first surely known in Louis Philippe's Galerie Espagnole at the Louvre in 1838. The self-taught artist has chosen to show the moment of deepest suffering or death.

Jean Baptiste Greuze
1725–1805, French

Comte d'Angiviller
  Oil on canvas
  25¼ x 21¼ in.
  Gift of Edith C. Blum (et al.), executors, in memory of Mr. and Mrs. Albert Blum, 66.28.1

The Comte d'Angiviller was, in succession to Marigny and for Louis XVI, director of the royal buildings, the minister for culture. This portrait was in the Salon of 1763; an exact copy, less finely drawn, is in the museum of Metz.

François Boucher
1703–1770, French

Virgin and Child with St. John and Angels
  Oil on canvas
  16⅛ x 13⅝
  Gift of Adelaide Milton de Groot in memory of the de Groot and Hawley families, 66.167

This small late painting, dated 1765, is exceptionally brisk and brilliant. As usual, there is great bravura and plenty of reference to the Italian "old masters" (Castiglione and Correggio are especially noticeable). At the very center of this artistry, however, there is the brilliant truth of the Child's face.

Ferdinand Victor Eugène Delacroix
  1798–1863, French

Basket of Flowers
  Oil on canvas
  42¼ x 56 in.
  Bequest of Miss Adelaide Milton de Groot
    (1876–1967), 67.187.60

Delacroix worked on five flower pieces from autumn, 1848, to spring, 1849, and attempted to exhibit all of them in the Salon of 1849. Three were withdrawn, leaving this and one now in Philadelphia. The Metropolitan also has a pastel study of this one.

Vincent Van Gogh
  1853–1890, Dutch

Portrait of the Artist; Potato Peeler
  Oil on canvas
  16 x 12½ in.
  Bequest of Miss Adelaide Milton de Groot
    (1876–1967), 67.187.70

These paintings are on the front and back of one small canvas. The *Potato Peeler* is earlier, from the Neunen period. In 1886, in Paris, Van Gogh painted himself in a straw hat, in a divisionistic technique, each stroke of which is as alive as wind and stars.

Paolo Veneziano
Active 1333–d. 1358/62, Italian (Venetian)

Madonna and Child Enthroned
Tempera on wood, gold on ground
32¼ x 19¾ in.
Bequest of Edward Fowles, 1971.115.5

A late work by this founder of Venetian painting,
datable to 1350 or slightly later, this ideally combines the Byzantine and Gothic. A green parrot
perches on the Madonna's hand: a symbol of the
virgin birth of Christ.

Annibale Carracci
1560–1609, Italian (Bolognese)

The Coronation of the Virgin
Oil on canvas
46⅜ x 55⅝ in.
Purchase, Bequest of Miss Adelaide Milton de
Groot (1876–1967) and Dr. and Mrs. Manuel
Porter and Sons Gift in honor of Mrs. Sarah
Porter, 1971.155

One of the most famous paintings of the greater
Bolognese "reformer," this picture was painted
around 1596 (shortly after Annibale's arrival in
Rome) for Cardinal Aldobrandini, the nephew
of the reigning pope. The sense of Correggio and
the nobility of Raphael—classical artists then almost a century old—happily combine to produce
a compact grandiloquence, which itself remained
for two centuries the classic of European painting.

Hilaire Germain Edgar Degas
1834–1917, French

The Dance Lesson
Pastel on paper
25 7/16 x 22 3/16 in.
Anonymous Gift, The H. O. Havemeyer Collection, 1971.185

One of Degas's most important pastels, this
painting was given in memory of the great collector and benefactress, Mrs. Havemeyer, who once
owned it. Especially large, it was made of three
sheets of paper glued together. A preparatory
drawing for the violinist is also in the Museum.

Abraham van Beyeren
1620–1690, Dutch

Still Life with Lobster and Fruits
Oil on wood
38 x 31 in.
Anonymous gift, 1971.254

A Ming porcelain bowl, a Nuremberg silver-gilt cup of about 1600, a tazza of the same period, a pocket watch (symbolizing temperance) are the works of art featured in this picture about expensive delicacies and other trappings of pleasure and privilege. Meaning: "Enjoy but Beware."

Jacob Pynas
Active about 1597–1648, Dutch

Paul and Barnabas at Lystra
Oil on wood
19 x 28⅞ in.
Gift of Emile Wolf, 1971.255

The young Rembrandt studied with Pynas, who himself had learned his carefully and classically conceived, emphatic style in Rome. In this picture, the Disciples are protesting because the impressed Lystrans are worshiping them as gods.

Abraham Bloemaert
1564–1651, Dutch

Moses Striking the Rock
Oil on canvas
31⅜ x 42½ in.
Gift of Mary V. T. Eberstadt, by exchange, 1972.171

In this 1596 work, the Dutch mannerist puts the subject of the picture in the shadow at the back while a crowd of bystanders show, in various forms of undress, and the most dramatic, elegant, and mannered of poses, a charade of the agonies of thirst and the pleasures of slaking it.

Paulus Bor
About 1600–1669, Dutch

The Enchantress
Oil on canvas
61¼ x 44¼ in.
Gift of Ben Heller, 1972.261

Italianate, earthy, enigmatic, and amusing, this picture may be an allegory of sloth, melancholy, and magic. A rather burned-out enchantress seems to have failed with her burnt offering. Her glum face reappears in the statue of Diana behind her and in the relief of the sphinx at right; or did the Utrecht artist regard all women as this stubbornly bitter?

Andrea Schiavone
1522(?)–1563, Italian (Venetian)

The Marriage of Cupid and Psyche
Oil on wood
51½ x 61⅞ in.
Purchase, Gift of Mary V. T. Eberstadt, by exchange, 1973.116

Cupid and Psyche take their marriage wreath and ring from Jupiter; the other gods shown are Juno, Mars, Venus, Hebe, a river god, and Vesta. The picture was made as a ceiling decoration in the Castello San Salvatore of Collato about 1550. It was originally an octagonal panel; its small, angled corners were added in the eighteenth century.

Francesco Del Cairo
1640–1665, Italian (Milanese)

Herodias
Oil on canvas
29¾ x 24¾ in.
Gift of Paul Ganz in memory of Rudolf Wittkower, 1973.165

Del Cairo shows mystical or orgasmic ecstasy with an exceptionally loving—sometimes perhaps perverse—realism. Lombardy, which produced Caravaggio, is famous for its realists, but few painters carried it to such a degree of immediacy and shock value.

Paris Bordon
1500–1571, Italian (Venetian)

Portrait of a Man in Armor with Two Pages
Oil on canvas
46 x 62 in.
Gift of Charles Wrightsman, 1973.311.1

In Venice, Bordon was a pupil of Titian, a rival of Lotto, and a source for Tintoretto and El Greco. This thoughtful portrait of a general, helped with his armor on the field of battle by white and black pages, is signed and must date to the 1540s. It may have been painted in Milan and could show a local potentate, Carlo da Rho.

Guercino (Giovanni Francesco Barbieri)
1591–1666, Italian (Bolognese)

The Vocation of San Luigi Gonzaga
Oil on canvas
140 x 106 in.
Gift of Charles Wrightsman, 1973.311.3

Born an important Italian noble, Gonzaga gave up his title (the crown on the floor) to practice exemplary piety and chastity (the lilies); his cult became that of a perfectly pure and model youth. Guercino painted this altarpiece for the Theatine church at Guastalla (where a later relative of the saint was reigning duke) in 1650.

Nicolas de Largillière
1656–1746, French

André François Alloys de Theys d'Herculais
Oil on canvas
54¼ x 41½ in.
Gift of Charles Wrightsman, 1973.311.4

D'Herculais was thirty-five when he was painted in 1727. This tough, determined young man—a rich, powerful, landed bourgeois—is shown ready for war. The armor belonged to Largillière; it is not what d'Herculais had used several years before in Spain, in the battle shown at right with a drama worthy of the nineteenth century.

Jacques de Gheyn the Elder
1565–1629, Dutch

Vanitas
Oil on wood
32½ x 21¼ in.
Charles B. Curtis, Marquand, Victor Wilbour Memorial, and Alfred N. Punnett Endowment Funds, 1974.1

The philosophers of laughter and tears, Democritus and Heracleitus, are shown in relief over a classical niche, dominated by a skull. The skull rests on ("all flesh is") grass and sits under a bubble, the surface of which reflects symbols of suffering and redemption (and is itself a symbol of human frailty and vanity). Cut flowers, vain riches, and a final plume of smoke complete the ensemble. Painted in 1603, this is perhaps the earliest Vanitas still life.

Sebastien Bourdon
1616–1671, French

The Baptism of Christ
Oil on canvas
59¾ x 46½ in.
Purchase, George Delacorte, Jr., Gift, 1974.2

Remembering the intellectual grandeur of Poussin, whose work Bourdon has just seen in Rome, and admiring not less the work of his Dutch and Flemish contemporaries, the artist has nevertheless invented an art sharply prefiguring the eighteenth century. Bourdon's *Baptism* was painted at the midpoint of the seventeenth century.

Jean Baptiste Camille Corot
1796–1875, French

Honfleur: Calvary
Oil on canvas
11¾ x 16⅛ in.
Purchase, Mr. and Mrs. Richard J. Bernhard Gift, 1974.3

Painted on a small panel shortly after Corot's return from Italy, this early landscape shows the artist's clear eye, accuracy of tone, and purity of heart.

Frederick Richards Lee
1798–1879, English

Garibaldi's Castle at Caprera
Oil on canvas
34¼ x 54⅝ in.
Gift of Dr. and Mrs. Melvin Goldberg, 1974.159

This beautiful Mediterranean scene shows the villa on the Straits of Corsica to which the Italian patriot retired and where he died. A royal academician, most of whose landscapes are British, the painter was a careful traditionalist. The vivacious southern climate appears to have inspired Lee with exceptional freshness and strength.

Jan Brueghel the Elder
1568–1625, Flemish

Woodland Road with Travelers
Oil on wood
18⅛ x 32¾ in.
Fletcher, Rogers, Pfeiffer, Dodge, Harris Brisbane Dick, and Louis V. Bell Funds and Joseph Pulitzer Bequest, 1974.293

Few paintings by "Velvet" Brueghel are in as perfect condition as this exquisite, large panel, which is signed and dated 1607 at lower left. A founder of seventeenth-century landscape painting, Jan Brueghel painted the *Woodland Road* forty-two years after his father, Pieter, painted the Metropolitan's *Harvesters*.

Guido Reni
1575–1642, Italian (Bolognese)

Allegory of Charity
Oil on canvas
54 x 41¾ in.
Gift of Charles Wrightsman, 1974.348

The virtue Charity is shown with three baby boys; one at her breast, one satisfied and asleep, one demanding his turn. Charity wears a rose red dress, to remind one of Christ's sacrificial blood. The painting has the great brilliance and ease of Guido's work of about 1630, at which time it apparently was bought from the artist by the founder of the great Liechtenstein collection.

Far Eastern Art

Comments by Marilyn Fu and Julia Meech-Pekarik, Assistant Curators (MF, JM-P), Martin Lerner, Research Fellow (ML), Suzanne G. Valenstein, Assistant Curator (SGV), and Jean Mailey, Associate Curator, Textile Study Room (JM)

Ch'ü Ting
Active about 1023–1056, Chinese (Northern Sung dynasty)

Handscroll: "Summer Mountains"
Ink and light color on silk
17¾ x 45¼ in. (sight)
Gift of The Dillon Fund, 1973.120.1

A magnificent vision of nature's vast riches, captured on a few feet of silk from China's classical period of landscape. We traverse the soaring mountains and winding paths, view the tumbling waterfalls and rising mists, and rest at the palatial inns in serene contemplation, as if on a pilgrimage.   MF

Li T'ang
Active about 1120-1140, Chinese (Southern Sung dynasty)

Handscroll: Marquis Wen-kung of Chin Recovering his State
Text written by the Sung emperor Kao-tsung (reigned 1127–1162)
Ink and color on silk
11⅞ in. x 28 ft.
Gift of The Dillon Fund, 1973.120.2

One of the most important early narrative figure paintings extant, illustrating in successive scenes an event of the fourth century B.C. The figures, drawn large in an archaistic manner befitting the drama, are handsomely integrated within the complex architectural and landscape settings. Innovative and fully conceived, the work of a grand master.   MF

Ma Ho-chih

Active about 1130–1170, Chinese (Southern Sung dynasty)

Handscroll: Odes of the State of Pin, from the Kuo-feng section of the "Book of Odes"
Text written in the style of the Sung emperor Kao-tsung (reigned 1127–1162)
Ink and color on silk
13⅞ in. x 24 ft.
Gift of J. Pierpont Morgan, by exchange, 1973.121.3

Seven illustrations of a classic text, executed with charm and a subtly modulated brush style, exemplifying the pictorial imagery of a highly poetic painter.   MF

Ma Lin

Active about 1250, Chinese (Southern Sung dynasty)

Album leaf: Orchids
Artist's signature on bottom edge
Ink and color on silk
10 5/16 x 8 13/16 in. (sight)
Gift of The Dillon Fund, 1973.120.10

One of the earliest and loveliest Sung flower paintings in existence. This delicate, rarefied view of nature epitomized thirteenth-century court taste.   MF

Chao Meng-chien

1199–1267 (?), Chinese (Southern Sung dynasty)

Handscroll: Narcissi
Ink on paper
13½ in. x 12¼ ft.
Gift of The Dillon Fund, 1973.120.4

One of the rare monochromatic scrolls on paper from this early period. The cool, fragrant essence of the flowers is captured in a pure style that invites analogy with music and architecture. The narcissus was a specialty of this poet-painter, a member of the Sung royal family.   MF

Hanging scroll: Jizō
   Japanese (late Kamakura period, early 14th c.)
   Color and gold on silk
   72 x 24¾ in.
   Gift of John M. Crawford, Jr., 69.139

During the Japanese Middle Ages (thirteenth-sixteenth centuries), Jizō's power to descend even into hell to rescue sinners contributed to his exceptional popularity. The Bodhisattva, dressed as a monk and holding a staff and sacred jewel, here descends toward the believer on a cloud, an iconography typical of salvationist Buddhist sects of the period.   JM-P

Hanging scroll: Aizen Myō-ō
   Japanese (Kamakura period, 14th c.)
   Color and gold on silk
   88 x 39⅜ in.
   Purchase, Mary Griggs Burke Gift, 66.90

Aizen Myō-ō, the King of Passion, is one of the many wrathful deities of Esoteric Buddhism. His demonic aspect is suggested by the scowling mouth, the menacing lion's head, the six arms brandishing weapons, and symbolic Buddhist attributes such as the bell and *vajra*, or thunderbolt. His body is always painted a deep red.

                                                    JM-P

Kanō Tsunenobu

1636–1713, Japanese (Edo period, late 17th-early 18th c.)

Two Albums: Copies of paintings by Chinese and Japanese masters
Color and ink on silk
Each leaf 16¾ x 11¼ in.
Gifts of Mr. and Mrs. Harry Rubin, 1972.213, 1974.224

Each painting bears Tsunenobu's signature and seal as well as the name of the painter whose work he has copied. Tsunenobu was a pupil of the great Kanō Tanyu, founder of the official Kanō school in Edō (Tokyo). The Kanō artists were patronized by government officials whose taste tended toward edifying Chinese subject matter.   JM-P

Kusumi Morikage

About 1700, Japanese (Edo period)

Pair of six-fold screens: The West Lake
Ink and light color on paper
68¾ in. x 12 ft. 2⅜ in.; 69 in. x 12 ft. 2⅜ in.
Purchase, Joseph Pulitzer Bequest, 1972.179.1,2

The West Lake, not far from Shanghai, was famous for its scenic beauty, and when Japanese Buddhist monks who had studied in the region introduced views of the lake to Japan, they became a favorite subject there. Little is known about Morikage, an independent artist who worked in a wide variety of styles. Most of his works are landscapes referring to classical Chinese masters.   JM-P

Matsumura Goshun
1752–1811, Japanese (Edo period)

Hanging scroll: Cat and Poems
Ink and color on paper
74½ x 15 13/16 in.
Rogers Fund, 1971.190

Famous as both a *haiku* poet and *haiga* artist, Goshun was a favored pupil of the great eighteenth-century Chinese-style literati-painter, Yosa Buson. The large inscription, a variation on a quotation by the twelfth-century poet Saigyō, reads "Everything human is Saigyō's cat." Three poems were inscribed by Nishiyama Chogetsu (1714–1801), Ozawa Gencha (1723–1801), and Ban Sukeyoshi.   JM-P

Standing Buddha
Northern India (first half 7th c.)
Bronze
H. 18½ inches
Purchase, Bequest of Florance Waterbury, 69.222

Dating to the late Gupta period, this image is stylistically dependent on forms developed in Uttar Pradesh and Madhya Pradesh during the sixth century. Tall and elegant, with a large, powerful head, this type of north Indian sculpture played a major role in the formulation of the early Nepali style. Indeed, part of the long history of this particular bronze was a stay of unknown duration in Nepal.   ML

Padmapani Lokeshvara seated in meditation
First half 7th c., Pakistani, Swat Valley region (or Kashmir)
Gilded bronze inlaid with silver and copper
H. 8¾ in.
Harris Brisbane Dick and Fletcher Funds, 1974.273

This superb sculpture, one of the finest and earliest Swat Valley bronzes known, closely reflects the inspiration of the Gupta idiom of northern India during the sixth century. It occupies a pivotal position in Indian art, illustrating the transition between the sixth-century Gupta style and the great sculptural traditions of the eighth century in Kashmir and the Swat Valley region.   ML

Four-armed Avalokiteshvara
>About second quarter 8th c., Thai, Mon-
> Dvaravati period, style of Central Thailand
>Bronze, eyes inlaid with silver and black glass
> or obsidian
>H. 56 in.
>Rogers Fund, 67.234

In 1964 a group of Buddhist bronzes was discovered at Pra Kon Chai, Buriram Province,
Thailand. Reflecting Cambodian, Indian, and
Mon-Dvaravati influences in an unequal admix-
ture, they are the mature products of important
workshops with obvious connections to Shri Deb
and Lopburi, major centers for sculpture production in central Thailand. This piece is the largest
and one of the finest of the trove.　　　ML

Kneeling Queen
>About mid-11th c., Cambodian, Angkor period,
> Baphuon style
>Bronze with traces of gold, eyes inlaid with
> silver
>H. about 17 in.
>Purchase, Bequest of Joseph H. Durkee, by
> exchange, 1972.147

This may well be the single most beautiful Khmer
bronze outside Cambodia. Magnificently poised
and balanced, the forms and volumes blend har-
moniously at every viewing angle. It was once
part of what must have been a spectacular bronze
group, produced by imperial workshops and
housed in one of the temples at the great Angkor
complex.　　　ML

Shalabanjika
>About mid-13th c., Indian, Orissa (Eastern
> Ganga dynasty)
>Perhaps from Surya Temple at Konarak
>H. 42½ in.
>Rogers Fund, 65.108

Integrated into the sculptural schema of the façades of Indian temples are a host of seductive
females whose identifications are not always apparent. Some are associated with nature's material bounties; others serve as demigod-consorts
and companions to the gods. The trunk of a tree
curving behind her, a blossoming branch in her
hand, this is probably one of the former. The
attenuated elegance of eleventh/twelfth-century
styles has here been replaced by a heavier system
of proportions.　　　ML

Mithuna: Loving couple
> About mid-13th c., Indian, Orissa (Eastern Ganga dynasty)
> Probably from Surya Temple at Konarak
> Stone
> H. 6 ft.
> Purchase, Bequest of Florance Waterbury, 1970.44

This heroic-sized couple, sexually less explicit than a good deal of the sculpture on the façades of the temple at Konarak, is carved almost in the complete round. The complexity of the interlocking volumes and negative spaces, molded by the hot Orissan sun, resulted in infinite visual variations.   ML

Gopis beseeching Krishna to return their stolen clothing
> About 1560, Indian, said to have been painted around Delhi
> From the so-called "Issarda" *Bhagavata Purana*
> Ink and colors on paper
> 7 9/16 x 10⅛ in.
> Gift of The H. Rubin Foundation, Inc., 1972.260

During the first half of the sixteenth century, a new style of painting developed in central and northern India, marked by a considerable freedom from foreign influences and earlier Indian styles and featuring bold, flat color and dramatic color combinations, charming abstractions of nature, fairy-tale systems of perspective, and an emphasis on the Krishna legend. This page, with its bold composition, delightful abstraction of floral forms, and appealing subject, is a superb example of the style.   ML

Bowl
> 1723–1735, Chinese (Ch'ing dynasty, Yung-cheng mark and period)
> Porcelain painted in overglaze enamels (*famille rose*)
> D. 4½ in.
> Bequest of Rosina H. Hoppin, Alfred W. Hoyt Collection, 65.86.12

A superb example of Ch'ing-dynasty porcelain decorated in the "Chinese taste."   SGV

Flask
  About 9th c., Chinese (T'ang dynasty)
  Stoneware with suffused glaze
  H. 11½ in.
  Gift of Mr. and Mrs. John R. Menke, 1972.274

An exceptionally fine example of the T'ang-dynasty wares with suffused glazes; possibly from the Huang-tao kilns in Chia Hsien, Honan Province.   SGV

Vase
  About mid-18th c., Chinese (Ch'ing dynasty)
  Porcelain with relief decoration under celadon
    glaze
  H. 20¾ in.
  Gift of Mr. and Mrs. Hugh J. Grant, 1974.223

An outstanding example of the celadon-glazed porcelain produced during the Ch'ing dynasty.
                                                   SGV

Monteith
  Early 18th c., Chinese (Ch'ing dynasty, later
    K'ang-hsi period)
  Porcelain painted in overglaze enamels (*famille
    verte*)
  L. 21¾ in.
  Gift of Mrs. Harry Payne Bingham, 1974.369.8

A splendid piece of export porcelain, combining a totally foreign shape with strictly Chinese decorative motifs.   SGV

Plate
    1426–1435, Chinese (Ming dynasty, Hsüan-te
      mark and period)
    Porcelain painted in underglaze blue
    D. 8⅛ in.
    Gift of Mrs. Richard E. Linburn in memory of
      Richard E. Linburn, 1975.99

Illustrates early fifteenth-century brushwork at
its best.   SGV

*Ceremonial coverlet in kimono shape with lob-
ster, rope, mandarin oranges; crest of three cloves*
    19th c., Japanese
    Cotton tabby, resist-dyed and painted with
      dyes and gouache
    L. at center back 5 ft. 3½ in.
    Seymour Fund, 66.239.3

Such coverlets were wadded with cotton and
used instead of a futon on special occasions. The
lobster and mandarin oranges, used in connection
with the New Year's celebration, imply a wish for
longevity.   JM

*Kimono ornamented with various diapers, wave
border*
    19th c., Japanese, northern Honshu
    Indigo-dyed cotton tabby embroidered with
      heavy white cotton yarn
    L. at center back 50¾ in.
    Seymour Fund, 67.172.1

Counted stitching like this, found in certain
groups of country cottons, strengthens the ground
fabric as well as decorating it.   JM

Four robes for lay aristocrats made from early Ch'ing-style dragon-robe silks from China
  Early 20th c., Tibetan
  L. at center back 60½, 58½, 55, 57½ in.
  Louis V. Bell Fund and Purchase, Bequest of Florance Waterbury, 68.45, 1971.61.1–3

Men of rank wore such robes at festivals like the New Year's celebration. Like these, many were of dragon satins from China received in return for tribute. The precious fabrics were stored in the treasure house attached to each household of means, and robes were made up from this store as needed. The dragon-robe tradition continued in Tibet even after the fall of the Manchu dynasty in China (1911). JM

Woman's over-robe with poem books and mandarin orange branches
  18th c., Japanese
  White satin damask, stitch and tie-dyed, couched with wrapped gold threads, embroidered with colored silks
  L. at center back 70 in.
  Gift of Mr. and Mrs. Earl Morse, 1972.18

A great lady must have trailed this formal over-robe from her shoulders while its padded hem moved gracefully behind her. The combination of many techniques to realize the graceful allusive ornament is typically Japanese.   JM

Panel (from a larger hanging) with imperial dragon and flaming pearl
  17th c., Chinese
  Silk gauze, embroidered with silks, couched with wrapped gold thread and wrapped peacock-feather filament thread
  41 x 16⅜ in.
  Gift of Bloomingdale's, 1972.36

The flaming pearl, pursued or grasped or swallowed by the dragon, is sometimes labeled with the character for "moon," suggesting the dragon's ancient background as a constellation shifting in the sky with the changing seasons, in relation to the waxing and waning moon.   JM

Panel with eight Manchurian cranes among clouds
  1662–1722, Chinese (K'ang-hsi period)
  Black satin damask with spaced rib, patterned with clouds and embroidered with silk flosses in white, black, shades of red, orange, yellow, blue, green.
  63 x 56½ in.
  Rogers Fund, 1972.75

Manchurian cranes are a symbol of longevity as well as the insignia of the first civil rank of the official hierarchy. This square is probably part of a set already in the collection (30.75.105), which has a pair of imperial hangings with gold dragons embroidered in the same style on the same distinctive ground.   JM

Robe for lay aristocrat made from Chinese imperial dragon robe of Yung-chêng period
    18th c., Tibetan
    Embroidered satin
    L. at center back 56 in.
    Purchase, Mr. and Mrs. Jerome A. Straka Gift
        and Rogers Fund, 1972.131

In 1694 the three heads of the Lama church were
permitted to receive imperial five-clawed dragon
satins in return for their tribute; apparently they
occasionally received actual dragon robes like
this one.   JM

Panel from hanging scroll: flowering trees rising
behind blue rock
    18th c., Chinese
    Warp twill, embroidered in silk flosses in white,
        shades of blue, green, ochre, pink
    49⅜ x 25½ in.
    Purchase, Mr. and Mrs. Jerome A. Straka Gift
        and Rogers Fund, 1973.8

Embroidery was sometimes a more expressive
medium than paint for rendering the sheen of
flower petals, the glossiness of leaves—favorite
subjects in the Far East.   JM

Dragon robes
> 18th c., Chinese
> Silk and metal tapestry, double-faced embroi-
>   dery on gauze, unlined
> L. at center back 57; 54½ in.
> Bequest of the Comtesse de Richelieu in mem-
>   ory of Captain Frederick May Wise, U.S.N.,
>   1973.28.2–3

This type of formal robe was introduced into China by the Manchus, and the cut is based on the riding coats of those mounted nomads from the steppes. The prescribed ornament symbolizes the universe: the wave border with spaced rocks, mountains, water, and land; the heavens, full of clouds, set with dragons representing cosmic force, at home in all elements.   JM

Fragment of compound weave with fantastic birds and animals
> 13th–14th c., Chinese (?)
> Silk warp twill patterned in gold leaf on mem-
>   brane strips
> 9 5/16 x 6½ in.
> Gift of Mrs. Howard J. Sachs in memory of
>   Arthur Upham Pope, 1973.269

This piece was found in Ispahan. A similarly woven silk with a lotus pattern in flat gold was found in Italy among the tomb vestments of Pope Benedict (d. 1304). Such silks, probably made somewhere in the vast Mongol empire, were the inspiration for the beautiful chinoiserie patterns of the medieval silks of Italy.   JM

Greek and Roman Art

Comments by   Dietrich von Bothmer, Chairman of the Department

Marble grave relief
  Greek (Attic), 2nd half of 4th c. B.C.
  H. 1.375 m.
  Harris Brisbane Dick Fund, 65.11.11

The sculpture had been in this country for thirty-five years and was "rediscovered" in a warehouse. It was a unique opportunity that was promptly seized.

Marble statuette of a woman
  Cycladic, 3rd millennium B.C.
  H. 62.8 cm.
  Gift of Christos G. Bastis, 68.148

Upper part of a marble statuette of a woman
  Cycladic, 3rd millennium B.C.
  H. 22.5 cm.
  Gift of Alastair Bradley Martin, 1971.258.1

Prices of Cycladic art have risen rapidly since World War II. We are therefore grateful for the gifts of these objects.

Bronze tripod leg
  Greek, mid-7th C. B.C.
  H. 89.7 cm.
  Purchase, Huntley Bequest, 58.11.6a–d, 59.11.1

A fragment of an especially elaborate tripod. The legs were hammered out of sheet bronze with the edges bent back at right angles to assure greater rigidity. The entire leg was then faced with a long bronze strip that bore incised decoration in panels, separated by a broad ornamental band. Two of the panels are preserved: their subject matter is taken from Greek mythology (Peleus and Thetis; Bellerophon battling the Chimaera).

Bronze funnel with strainer
  Etruscan, 6th C. B.C.
  L. 33 cm.
  Rogers Fund, 65.11.1

A typical Etruscan utensil used at banquets and a welcome addition to our large and important Etruscan collection.

Bronze oinochoe
  Greek, 5th C. B.C.
  H. 22.6 cm.
  Rogers Fund, 1970.11.1

Bronze oinochoai share some of the sculptural adjuncts with bronze hydriai. We had long wanted such an oinochoe and were lucky to obtain one at public auction in New York.

Bronze hydria with lid
  Greek, 3rd c. B.C.
  H. 49.5 cm.
  Rogers Fund, 66.11.12

Bronze hydria
  Greek, 6th c. B.C.
  H. 42 cm.
  Harris Brisbane Dick Fund, 67.11.7

Our collection of Greek bronze hydriai is the biggest in the world outside Athens. A conscious effort has been made to show the development of the shape over the centuries. Thus an archaic hydria and a Hellenistic one are essential to the understanding of the class.

Bronze statuette of a woman
  Etruscan, 4th–3rd c. B.C.
  H. 21.5 cm.
  Edith Perry Chapman Fund, 65.11.9

Richly dressed and bedecked with jewelry, this figure reveals how in Etruria the older conventions of classic Greek art linger on long after they have been replaced in Greece by the new mood and spirit of the Hellenistic age.

Bronze portrait of a boy
  Roman, 1st c.
  H. 29.2 cm.
  Purchase, funds from various donors, 66.11.5

The bust was probably attached to a marble herm. Some have seen in this portrait the emperor Nero as a child.

Bronze statuette of Hermes
  Late Hellenistic–early Roman, 1st c. B.C.–1st c.
  H. 29.1 cm.
  Rogers Fund, 1971.11.11

By the end of the fourth century B.C. Greek statues had attained the stance and proportions that we call classic, and the idealized renderings of gods and goddesses, athletes and heroes, continued to be admired and copied for many centuries. The perfect proportions of this Hermes are echoed in other portrayals of the god. Especially well preserved, this large statuette counts among the finest.

Bronze statuette of man in artisan's dress
  Greek (Hellenistic), 1st c. B.C.
  H. 40.3 cm.
  Rogers Fund, 1972.11.1

In its search for new subjects the Hellenistic age discovered the common man, and coupled with the realism introduced in sculpture at that time, the artists of the period took delight in rendering the human form in all its aspects, not just the beautiful forms and proportions of the classic period. Thus a humble artist or artisan with his sketch pad tucked into his belt is shown in a pensive mood. The possibility that this is the portrait of a living artist cannot be excluded.

Bronze head of a griffin
  Greek, 7th c. b.c.
  H. 25.8 cm.
  Bequest of Walter C. Baker, 1972.118.54

This head is among the earliest cast in cire-perdue. It is said to have been found in Olympia, and together with two others must once have decorated a bowl set on a tripod.

Bronze support: woman wearing peplos
  Greek, 6th c. b.c.
  H. 19.5 cm.
  Bequest of Walter C. Baker, 1972.118.57

Many of the finest Greek bronze statuettes were sculptural adjuncts to utensils. This standing woman served as a support for an incense burner.

Statuette of a youth
  Greek, 6th c. b.c.
  H. 15.2 cm.
  Bequest of Walter C. Baker, 1972.118.101

One of the finest of all archaic bronze statuettes, this kouros shows a certain affinity with bronzes that have been found on the East Greek island of Samos.

Statuette of a hunter with cap
  Greek, 5th c. b.c.
  H. 14 cm.
  Bequest of Walter C. Baker, 1972.118.71

This powerful statuette of a nude man resembles in its attitude that of a Herakles or a warrior. The left hand may have held a bow.

Mirror supported by woman holding a bird
  Greek, 5th c. b.c.
  H. 40.4 cm.
  Bequest of Walter C. Baker, 1972.118.78

This splendid mirror is exceptionally well preserved and forms a welcome pendant to a Greek mirror of the same class given in 1917 by J.P. Morgan. It illustrates most forcefully the desire of supreme Greek craftsmen to add even to ordinary utensils sculptural shapes that, separately and independently, would rank as masterpieces.

Statuette of a dancing youth
  Greek, late 4th–early 5th c. b.c.
  H. 20.1 cm.
  Bequest of Walter C. Baker, 1972.118.94

In the early Hellenistic age the human body began to be shown in movements not before attempted. The torsion of the body, coupled with the movement of arms and legs, characterizes this youth as a dancer.

Statuette of a veiled and masked dancer
    Greek, late 3rd c. B.C.
    H. 20.5 cm.
    Bequest of Walter C. Baker, 1972.118.95

Though dressed in two garments and veiled, this dancer reveals the movement of her body. There is no principal view; the figure should be admired in the round.

Bronze statuette of a warrior
    Etruscan, 5th c. B.C.
    H. 25.9 cm.
    Bequest of Walter C. Baker, 1972.118.53

In Etruscan art of the Umbrian hinterland a type of statuette of warriors was developed that perhaps served as votive offerings to the god of war.

Statuette of a satyr
    Etruscan, 5th c. B.C.
    H. 11.6 cm.
    Bequest of Walter C. Baker, 1972.118.72

The satyr wears the loincloth associated with the costume of the satyr-play, which in the Greek theater followed the performance of tragedies.

Bronze candelabrum
   Etruscan, 4th c. b.c.
   H. 53.3 cm.
   Bequest of Walter C. Baker, 1972.118.87

A fine Etruscan candelabrum in good condition is a great rarity. The interest of this object is further enhanced by the sculptural adjunct of the satyr Marsyas, shown tied to a tree following his defeat in the musical contest with Apollo.

Bronze mask of Silenus
   Roman, 1st c.
   H. 25.4 cm.
   Bequest of Walter C. Baker, 1972.118.98

This splendid handle attachment of a situla is of particular importance to the Museum, as a similar one had been given in 1958.

Gold pectoral
   Etruscan, 6th c. b.c.
   H. 33.7 cm.
   Fletcher Fund, 65.11.10

This rare and wonderful object was offered to the Museum by a Swiss collector and is said to have been found in northern Italy. There is only one other pectoral like it—in the Vatican. While the animals and ornaments are Etruscan in style, the shape of the pectoral is traditional in northern Europe.

Group of bronze and silver objects
  Greek, 4th and 3rd c. B.C.
  H. (situla) 62.8 cm.
  Bequest of Walter C. Baker, 1972.118.88,161–164

The four silver vases and bronze bucket were found together in Prusias (Asia Minor). In 1952 they appeared on the Munich market but were not bought by the Museum. Thanks to a great collector and friend, the late Walter C. Baker, this important group was acquired together and bequeathed to the Museum.

Group of 222 gold, silver, and bronze objects
  East Greek, 6th c. B.C.
  Illustrated: Rogers Fund, 68.11.11, 68.11.16

In the sixth century B.C. wealthy and powerful Greek cities flourished on the western and southern coast of Asia Minor, and even the Anatolian kingdoms of Lydia and Phrygia were largely Hellenized. The Persian conquest first of Lydia and then of the Greek cities did not eradicate the strong Greek influence in Asia Minor; rather, the skilled Greek artists found employment at the Persian court, and much of Persian art of the late sixth century betrays this indebtedness. Greek and Persian art became fused, and of the many objects among these treasures some are pure Greek in form and style while others are more Greek in style than in form. Together, these splendid objects reveal most forcefully the happy climate in which art flourished in spite of political differences.

Glass phiale
    Greek, late 6th c. B.C.
    D. 15.4 cm.
    Arthur Darby Nock Fund in memory of Gisela
      Richter, 69.11.6

This was offered to us as coming from the same area as one or two of our so-called East Greek treasures. As early glass is relatively rare, it is an important piece even without the link to the other objects.

One-handled kantharos: banquet of nine men, flute player
    Attic, late 6th c. B.C.
    Attributed to the Michigan Painter
    H. 29.0 cm.
    Rogers Fund, 63.11.4

Not all the Attic vases that were made in great numbers during the best centuries of Greek art represent the shapes that were invented and used in Attica. The one-handled kantharos belongs to a small number of shapes that were traditional in Etruria and were made in Attica chiefly to serve the Etruscan market. The class to which this vase belongs is a very small one; our example is particularly interesting in that one of the banqueters drinks from the very vessel represented by the vase.

Kalpis: Ajax and Achilles playing draughts
    Attic, about 500 B.C.
    Attributed to the Berlin Painter
    H. 36.4 cm.
    Purchase, Mr. and Mrs. Arnold Whitridge Gift,
      65.11.12

The Berlin Painter is one of the finest Attic artists of the late archaic period, and this hydria takes its place alongside other masterpieces by him in our collection.

Vase in the form of a jackdaw
   Etruscan, 4th c. B.C.
   H. 16.4 cm.
   Rogers Fund, 65.11.13

Although much of the fame of classical art rests on the superb achievement of rendering the human body in artistically satisfying forms, it should not be overlooked that the repertory of ancient artists also included animals. The conceit of using animals in the form of vases goes back to the Bronze Age and never really died out in Western art. This bird, bedecked with a collar and holding a jewel in its beak, is a superb example of Etruscan clay modeling. A rare object that enriches our appreciation of ancient art.

Stand: side A, Iris; B, Sphinx
   Attic, about 520 B.C.
   H. (as restored) 25.35 cm.
   Louis V. Bell Fund, 65.11.14

Even rarer than the one-handled kantharos is this stand of very special shape, an Attic elaboration of a shape known only in Etruscan pottery. With its mate (in the Schimmel collection), the pair is the only Attic example that has been discovered. It was made at a time of great experimentation, in the last quarter of the sixth century B.C., and in its technique and scheme of decoration it skillfully combines some features of Attic black figure, others of Attic red figure, and even introduces another dimension in the heads that are modeled in the round.

Kantharos: bull between lions
   Boeotian, 6th c. B.C.
   H. 18.1 cm.
   Rogers Fund, 66.11.2

This strengthens our collection of archaic vases made outside of Attica. While influenced by Attic vase-painting, the shape and the style of drawing are unmistakably Boeotian.

Column-krater
  Laconian, 6th c. B.C.
  H. 28.0 cm.
  Rogers Fund, 66.11.16

In the sixth century B.C. Laconian pottery developed its own shapes and style and was widely exported, in competition with Attic and Corinthian.

Bell-krater: side A, Tydeus, Aktaion, Theseus, and Castor; B, three youths
  Attic, last quarter of 5th c. B.C.
  Attributed to the Dinos Painter
  H. 40.6 cm.
  Gift of Christos G. Bastis, 66.79

This vase, which belonged to the king of the Two Sicilies, found its way to England in Napoleonic times. It reappeared in New York in the late forties and was rediscovered by Mr. Bastis.

Skyphos: side A, Athena with goose; B, Nike with bird and phiale
  Attic, about 470 B.C.
  Attributed to the Painter of the Yale Lekythos
  H. 8.2 cm.
  Rogers Fund, 67.11.23

In the early classic period much of the emphasis is on quiet groupings. The pegasos on the shield of Athena had been a favorite blazon on the Panathenaic prize amphorae by the Kleophrades Painter, painted about twenty-five years earlier.

Kalpis: man courting woman; man and seated woman
   Attic, about 500 B.C.
   Attributed to the Eucharides Painter
   H. 35.0 cm.
   Gift of Christos G. Bastis, 67.44.2

When the red-figured technique was introduced into Attic vase-painting, the older, black-figured technique continued for some time and some painters, like the Eucharides Painter, worked in both.

Pelike: side A, two musicians at table; B, flute player between two athletes
   Attic, about 520 B.C.
   H. 30.7 cm.
    Gift of Walter Bareiss and loan of Louvre C 11990, 68.27 and L. 68.121

The pelike is one of the "new" shapes introduced into the repertory of Attic vases in the last quarter of the sixth century. A fragment of this vase has been in the Campana collection of the Louvre since the 1860s; it has been lent to us for incorporation.

Vase in the shape of a hedgehog
   Corinthian, 6th c. B.C.
   H. 7.0 cm.
   Purchase, Winslow Carlton Gift, 69.11.3

This little perfume vase is another newcomer to our zoo.

Volute-krater: *Judgment of Paris*
    Apulian, 4th C. B.C.
    H. (overall) 77.0 cm.
    Purchase, Mrs. J. J. Rorimer Gift, 69.11.7

This important vase had been known for almost a century when it unexpectedly became available for purchase.

Lekanis
    Apulian, 4th C. B.C.
    D. 58.0 cm.
    Rogers Fund, 69.11.8

Many of our vases are acquired without precise knowledge of the tombs in which they may have been found, but from old records and publications it has sometimes been possible to identify certain tomb groups. This very large dish was recognized as having been found with vases of other shapes already in the collection and was promptly acquired when it became available.

Kylix: I, hoplitodrome; A–B, Thracians and horses
    Attic, about 500 B.C.
    Attributed to the Proto-panaetian Group
    Gift of Dietrich von Bothmer and loan of
        Louvre G 26 and G 26 bis, 69.44.1 and
        L. 1970.48

Early excavations in Etruria were often conducted in a hasty fashion with the result that fragments of vases found broken were scattered. Here, big fragments of a magnificent kylix were seen to join others that had been in the Louvre for over a hundred years. The pieces in the Louvre complete the composition.

Skyphos: side A, Judgment of Paris; B, ogre scaring three men
  Boeotian, late 5th–early 4th c. B.C.
  H. 22.0 cm.
  Purchase, Anonymous Gift, 1971.11.1

Greek vases abound in comic subjects, but caricatures do not begin until the late fifth century B.C. A certain class of Boeotian drinking vessels specializes in parodies of well-known myths. Here the subject is the Judgment of Paris, with Aphrodite, the winner of the contest, transformed into a hag.

Plate: Amazon carrying dead companion
  Attic, about 510 B.C.
  D. 12.2 cm.
  Gift of Alastair Bradley Martin, 1971.258.2

One of the choice pieces from the "private" collection of Joseph Brummer.

Oön (egg-shaped perfume vase): the abduction of Helen
  Attic, about 420–410 B.C.
  Near the Eretria Painter
  H. 5.1 cm.
  Gift of Alastair Bradley Martin, 1971.258.3

This has wafer-thin walls, and the delicacy of its construction is matched by the daintiness of its decoration. It is said to have been found with another egg, formerly in the collection of Mrs. Stathatou, now in the National Museum, Athens.

Calyx-krater: Sleep and Death lifting the body of Sarpedon
  Attic, about 515 B.C.
  Signed by Euxitheos as potter and Euphronios as painter
  H. 45.7 cm.
  Bequest of Joseph H. Durkee, Gift of Darius Ogden Mills, and Gift of Mr. and Mrs. C. Ruxton Love, by exchange, 1972.11.10

This is easily the museum's most important single purchase of the last ten years in the area of Greek and Roman art.

Vase in the form of a bull's head
  Late Minoan III or Mycenaean III, about 1425–1150 B.C.
  H. 9.5 cm.
  Gift of Alastair Bradley Martin, 1973.35

At the height of the Minoan civilization on Crete there was much commerce with the Greek mainland, so it is often hard to tell whether a vase was made on Crete by Minoan artists or in Greece proper by a Mycenaean. This powerful rhyton is said to have been found in Attica and may be either a Minoan import or a local product strongly influenced by Minoan style.

Kylix: banqueters
  Attic, about 470 B.C.
  Attributed to the Euaion Painter
  Gift of Dietrich von Bothmer and loan of Louvre C 11439, 1973.96.5 and L. 1973.16.1

The Euaion Painter, one of the most prolific followers of Douris, was poorly represented in the Museum. In the course of the last ten years fragments of a cup appeared on the market and were acquired piece by piece. When the cup was nearly completed it was discovered that a small triangular fragment was in the Louvre. This has now been incorporated.

Oinochoe
  Rhodian, 6th c. B.C.
  H. 15.3 cm.
  Purchase, Richard A. Van Avery Gift, 1974.11.2

In so rich a field as Greek pottery it is almost impossible to be representative in all areas, but by keeping constant watch it has been possible to round off the collection in the weakest areas. In the sixth century B.C. many local schools of pottery flourished outside Attica. This handsome mug (or jug) was made on the island of Rhodes and is decorated with characteristic East Greek patterns.

Phiale
  Attic, 6th c. B.C.
  D. 18.84 cm.
  Purchase, Helen H. Mertens Gift, 1973.11.3

Phiale decorated in Six's technique
  Attic, late 6th c. B.C.
  D. 19.5 cm.
  Purchase, Helen H. Mertens Gift, 1974.11.3

The purchase of a splendid gold phiale led to general study of the shape in metal and in pottery. The Museum lacked Attic phialai but within two years good examples appeared on the market and were promptly acquired. One of them is all black save for a tongue pattern around the omphalos; the other has a painted ivy wreath.

Oinochoe: centaur, eagle, and hare
  Attic, about 530 B.C.
  H. 23.9 cm.
  Arthur Darby Nock Fund in memory of Gisela
    Richter, 1974.11.4

Though somewhat fragmentary, this is of great
importance as one of the earliest vases painted
in the red-figured technique.

Islamic Art

Comments by   Marilyn Jenkins (MJ) and Marie Lukens Swietochowski (MLS), Associate Curators

Four demon figures
   Iran or Central Asia, 15th c.
   Colors and gold on silk
   L. 13½ in.
   Harris Brisbane Dick Fund, 68.175

Painting on silk reflects Chinese influence; the subject relates to Central Asian shamanism.   MLS

Hatifi

Manuscript of Khosrow and Shirin
   Turkey, dated 904 A.H./A.D. 1498/99
   Colors, ink, gold on paper
   Harris Brisbane Dick Fund, 69.27

Ottoman painting of this early date and of this quality, with its crisp pastel coloring and clarity of form, is rare. It is influenced by Persian painting, but the greater interest in perspective is a Turkish characteristic.   MLS

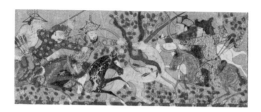

Leaves from a Shah-nameh
  Iran, early 14th c.
  Colors, gold, silver on paper
  Rogers Fund, 69.74.1–9

Details show the artistic influence brought from
the Far East by the Mongol conquerors of Iran,
but the overall decorative treatment is Persian.

MLS

Leaf from a Koran
  Egypt, 14th c.
  Paper
  Gift of Mr. and Mrs. Russell Pickering, 69.149

A departure from the usual Mamluk *Korans* in
that even the decorative heading, in white on a
gold ground, is written in a cursive script instead
of an archaizing Kufic.   MJ

Leaves from a Shah-nameh
  Iran (Tabriz), second quarter of 16th c.
  Colors, gold, silver on paper
  Gift of Arthur A. Houghton, Jr., 1970.301.1–76

Part of a manuscript of the *Shah-nameh* created
for Shah Tahmasp (reigned 1524–1576) during the
early part of his reign, with miniatures by the
leading artists of the day in a period of intense
cultural patronage and artistic achievement. MLS

Fragment of a giant Koran *page*
Iran (Herat), about 1430
Paper and ink
17¼ x 38¼ in.
Anonymous Gift, 1972.279

This page of vigorous thulth script is attributed to the Timurid prince Baysonghor and comes from a unique monumental *Koran*   MLS

Leaf from a Ragamala *depicting a Ragini*
India (Deccan), late 16th c.
Colors on paper
Rogers Fund, 1972.285.1

A charming example of the painting of the Deccani school, more lyrical in mood than Mughal court art of the same period.   MLS

Portrait of a kneeling youth
Iran (Qazvin), about 1580
Colors, ink, gold on paper
Rogers and Fletcher Funds, 1973.92

This miniature exemplifies the graceful, long-limbed figures of this elegant style of the Safavid court in the latter part of the sixteenth century.
      MLS

Muhammad Baqir

Fight between a lion and a dragon
  Iran, 17th c., signed
  Ink and colors on paper
  Rogers Fund, 1974.20

The calligraphic handling of the brush and the
interplay of textures and forms typical of the
period seem particularly effective in this drawing.
                                              MLS

Leaves from a Shah-nameh
  Iran, early 14th c.
  Colors, gold, silver on paper
  Bequest of Monroe C. Gutman, 1974.290.1–43

The miniatures from this unique manuscript,
like those of 69.74.1–9, have incorporated Mongol features (type of armor, textile patterns, etc.)
but here the approach of the artist is more fo-
cused on the action and human drama than on
the decorative elements. The *Shah-nameh,* while
incomplete, consists of binding, text pages, and
41 miniatures.   MLS

Manuscript with three miniatures of the Bustan of
Sa'di *written by Sultan Muhammad Nur*
  Iran or Uzbekistan, dated 920 A.H./A.D. 1514
  Purchase, Louis V. Bell Fund and The Vincent
    Astor Foundation Gift, 1974.294.1–4

The court style of Persian painting, brought to
such perfection by the Bihzad school of the
Timurid princes in Herat in the late fifteenth
century, continued into the sixteenth, especially
dominating painting in Bukhara at the court of
the Uzbek sultans.   MLS

Tiraz textile
  Egypt (Fatimid period), 10th c.
  Rogers Fund, 1971.151

This linen fabric, preserved in its complete length, with a silk tapestry-woven Kufic inscription, is of exceptional quality and size. The inscription tells that the textile was manufactured during the reign of the Fatimid caliph al-'Aziz and that it was made in a private factory in Tinnis in 983.
                                                           MJ

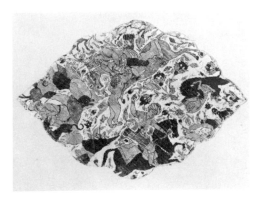

Tent panel
  Iran, 16th c.
  Cut velvet, silk, metal strips
  L. 23⅝ in.
  Fletcher Fund, 1972.189

The walls of royal tents were covered with rich, colorful panels like this one, often depicting heroic scenes.   MLS

Floral carpet
  Iran (Kurdistan), late 18th or early 19th c.
  Wool; Gördes knot
  22 ft. 10 in. x 8 ft. 10 in.
  Gift of Joseph V. McMullan, 68.219

Dense floral stem systems carry bold palmette, floral, and leaf motifs, which contrast admirably with the cartouche and hexagon shapes of the border.   MLS

Floral and arabesque carpet
 Iran (Herat or Isfahan), first half of 17th c.
 Wool; Senneh knot
 15 ft. 9 in. x 6 ft. 11 in.
 Rogers Fund, 69.244

A bold arabesque in light and dark blue dominates the underlying floral and stem system and
gives a marked change of rhythm to the stiffer
patterns in the border. MLS

Carpet
 Egypt, probably 1460–1490
 Wool; Senneh knot
 29 ft. 7 in. x 7 ft. 10 in.
 Fletcher Fund, 1970.105

Belongs to a group that combines contemporary
Egyptian motifs, such as geometrical patterns
and older pharaonic motifs such as the papyrus
plant with some that were typical for certain
classes of Coptic textiles. This example is unique
among Mamluk rugs in having five major units.
MJ

Garden and medallion carpet
 Iran (Kerman?), 17th c.
 Wool and cotton; Senneh knot
 6 ft. 9 in. x 4 ft. 8 in.
 Gift of Joseph V. McMullan, 1970.302.2

The designer has evoked the temporal and symbolic beauties of a garden with the display of
stylized floral plants. MLS

Medallion carpet
> Turkey (Ottoman court manufactory, probably
> Cairo), about 1600
> Wool; Senneh knot
> 6 ft. 6¾ in. x 4 ft. 4 in.
> Gift of Joseph V. McMullan, 1971.263.2

The wavy lines and discs were a favorite pattern
of the art of the Ottoman court; the medallions
imitate the layout of a Persian carpet.　　MLS

Prayer rug
> India, Mughal period, mid-17th c.
> Cotton, silk, wool; Senneh knot
> 5 ft. 1 in. x 3 ft. 4½ in.
> Bequest of Joseph V. McMullan, 1974.149.2

A rare example of a Mughal prayer rug with
typical seventeenth-century patterns in the foliate, cusped arch and a symmetrical but naturalistic floral plant in the field.　　MLS

Bottle
> Iran, 8th c.
> Silver-gilt
> H. 7 3/16 in.
> Pfeiffer Fund, 69.224

The allover repoussé design is in the beveled
style—a technique of decoration very popular in
early Islamic art in particular—in which background and foreground are equally important.
　　MJ

Dagger with ram's-head finial
  India, Mughal period, late 18th or early 19th c.
  Gold, diamonds, rubies, enamel
  L. 12 3/16 in.
  Rogers Fund, 1970.180

The Mughal-Indian taste for opulence is captured here. The art of the enameler, brought to its peak in this period, is seen in the purity and translucence of the colors.   MLS

Bowl
  Afghanistan (probably Ghazneh), 11th c.
  Bronze
  D. 15 5/16 in.
  Rogers Fund, 1971.42

Our largest and best-preserved piece of Ghaznavid metalwork, which is little known, this bowl is decorated inside with the much-favored motif of a royal reveler surrounded by entertainers.
                                                              MJ

Box
  Syria or Iraq, mid-13th c.
  Bronze
  H. 4⅛ in.
  Rogers Fund, 1971.39

One of a relatively rare group of medieval Islamic bronzes with Christian figures or scenes. Christ's entry into Jerusalem is depicted in one of the arcades.   MJ

Throne leg
 Iran, late 7th–early 8th c.
 Bronze
 H. 22 7/16 in.
 Purchase, Joseph Pulitzer Bequest, 1971.143

This griffin protoma represents a Muslim continuation of a pre-Islamic tradition: the symbolic identification of winged and particularly powerful animals with the royal person.   MJ

Mirror
 Iran, 16th c.
 Steel, inlaid with gold
 H. 9⅜ in.
 Fletcher Fund, 1972.24

With its delicate allover arabesque and floral pattern, a rare and exquisite piece of early Safavid metalwork.   MLS

Stucco figure
 Iran, 12th c.
 H. 57 in.
 Gift of Mr. and Mrs. Lester Wolfe, 67.119

For religious reasons figural sculpture never gained the popularity in the Islamic world that it held in most other cultures. Therefore, we were particularly fortunate to receive the gift of this rare, almost life-size, figure, which is similar to one that entered the collection in 1957.   MJ

Tabouret
  Iran, 12th c.
  Ceramic
  H. 13⅛ in.
  Purchase, Joseph Pulitzer Bequest, 69.225

In the shape of a pleasure pavilion, this was probably used as a low table to hold food and drink.   MJ

Paneled room from the Nur ad-Din House
  Syria (Damascus), dated 1119 A.H./A.D. 1707
  Gift of the Hagop Kevorkian Fund, 1970.170

The colored marble floor, the exquisitely decorated wooden walls and ceilings, and the ceramic tiles reflect the calm and graciousness of early eighteenth-century Syrian houses. This room is exceptional in the United States because of its completeness and superb condition.   MLS

Bracelet
  Iran, 10th or 11th c.
  Gold
  D. 4¾ in.
  Harris Brisbane Dick Fund, 65.51

Knowledge of medieval Islamic jewelry is limited, since relatively few objects have survived and most contain no inscribed information to permit a precise dating. Fortunately, this bracelet can be placed in a historical context by means of the inscription on a companion piece in the Walters Art Gallery, Baltimore.   MJ

Ring
　Egypt, Fatimid period, 11th c.
　Gold
　L. of bezel ⅝ in.
　Gift of Mr. and Mrs. J. J. Klejman, 1971.165

One of the rare few extant, this ring helps to fill out our collection of Fatimid jewelry.　MJ

Necklace
　Probably Iran, 8th–11th c.
　Gold and garnets
　D. of bead ⅞ in.
　Purchase, Hess Foundation Gift, 1972.188.2

The surfaces of the large beads (the small beads are not part of the original necklace) are decorated with tangent geometrical forms executed in gold rope and highlighted with gold granules.　MJ

Necklace
　Probably Iran, 8th–11th c.
　Gold
　D. of bead ⅞ in.
　Gift of Mrs. Jacob M. Kaplan, 1972.218.1

The construction and decoration of the large beads (the small beads are not part of the original necklace) resemble those of 1972.188.2.　MJ

Pendant
Egypt (Fatimid period), about 2nd quarter of
11th c.
Gold
H. 1¾ in.
The Friends of the Islamic Department Fund,
1974.22

The Fatimid craftsmen took their use of crescent-
shaped ornaments from Byzantine art. This
beautifully crafted pendant would have been
framed by strands of pearls or beads of precious
or semi-precious stones supported by the gold
loops still remaining.   MJ

Bowl
Iran, 10th c.
Ceramic
D. 18 in.
Rogers Fund, 65.106.2

Perhaps the most outstanding, as well as the
largest of the type in our collection, this bowl has
for its decoration an Arabic inscription in Kufic
script reading "Planning before work protects
you from regret. Prosperity and peace."   MJ

Plate
Iran, 16th c.
Ceramic, underglaze painted
D. 17¼ in.
Harris Brisbane Dick Fund, 65.109.2

Two dragons twisted in combat are shown on
stylized patterns for rocks and waves. The design
and colors are strongly influenced by those of
Chinese porcelain.   MLS

Candlestick
   Turkey (Iznik), early 16th c.
   Ceramic, underglaze painted
   H. 9⅜ in.
   Harris Brisbane Dick Fund, 66.4.1

The beautiful white body, blue decoration, and brilliant, colorless glaze are all characteristic of the earliest Iznik ware. This piece is inscribed "Its owner is Hajji Muhammad ibn Sulaiman."   MLS

Bowl with scalloped edge
   Turkey (Iznik), early 16th c.
   Ceramic, underglaze painted
   D. 14¼ in.
   Harris Brisbane Dick Fund, 66.4.2

The graceful floral scrolls and plants are of Persian origin, the peonies and lotuses of Chinese.
                                                          MLS

Chess set
   Iran, 12th c.
   Ceramic
   H. (largest piece) 2 3/16 in.
   Pfeiffer Fund, 1971.193 a–ff

The acquisition of this earliest extant Iranian set greatly enhances the Museum's large collection of sets and individual pieces from many different areas and periods.   MJ

Two ewers
  Iran, 12th–13th c.
  Ceramic
  H. (each) 13 in.
  Harris Brisbane Dick Fund, 66.175.3–4

Complete ewers of this size and quality of design and potting are rare. These are of typical Kashan design, which was not represented hitherto in our collection by outstanding examples.   MJ

Container supported by a quadruped
  Syria, 7th–8th c.
  Glass
  H. 4⅜ in.
  Gift of Mrs. Charles S. Payson, 69.153

Probably used to hold kohl, this is one of a group often called dromedary flasks.   MJ

Multilobed bowl
  Iran, 7th–9th c.
  Glass
  D. 5 7/16 in.
  Rogers Fund, 1970.20

Lobed vessels have a long tradition in Iranian art. This example has an apparently unique feature: horizontal, wheel-cut fluting on the interior of alternate lobes.   MJ

Beaker
  Iran or Iraq, late 9th c.
  Glass, relief-cut
  H. 5⅜ in.
  Rogers Fund and Jack A. Josephson, Dr. and Mrs. Lewis Balamuth, and Mr. and Mrs. Alvin W. Pearson Gifts, 1974.45

The decoration was created by cutting away the whole outer surface except for the design, which remains in relief—a technical tour de force in glass cutting.   MJ

Beaker
  Egypt or Iraq, 9th c.
  Glass, luster-painted
  H. 4⅛ in.
  Rogers Fund and Gifts of Richard S. Perkins, Mr. and Mrs. Charles Wrightsman, Mr. and Mrs. Louis E. Seley, Walter D. Binger, Margaret Mushekian, Mrs. Frances E. Keally, Hess Foundation, Mehdi Mahboubian, and Mr. and Mrs. Bruce J. Westcott, 1974.74

The technique of luster painting on glass probably originated in Egypt. Not long after its introduction it was used also to decorate pottery, a ninth-century adaptation that left a permanent imprint on the pottery industry not only in the Middle East but in Europe and America as well. This is the only complete example of luster-painted glass in the Museum's collection.   MJ

Medieval Art and The Cloisters

Medieval Art   Comments by Carmen Gomèz-Moreno, Curator (CG-M), Margaret E. Frazer, Associate Curator (MEF), and Charles T. Little, Assistant Curator (CTL)

The Cloisters   Comments by J. L. Schrader, Curator in Charge (JLS) and Jane Hayward, Curator (JH)

Design for a portal
  French, last quarter 15th c.
  Pen and brown ink on parchment
  17 9/16 x 11¾ in.
  The Cloisters Collection, 68.49

One of many to survive from the late Gothic period, this drawing is evidently one of a series of two for an interior side portal next to the ambulatory of a church—a portal in a position similar to that of the "Porte Rouge" of Notre Dame Cathedral in Paris.   JLS

The Apocalypse
  French (Normandy), about 1320
  Manuscript on vellum, illuminated
  12⅛ x 9 in.
  The Cloisters Collection, 68.174

The Apocalypse manuscript and two others of the same period (in London and Paris) appear to derive from a late-thirteenth-century English source. The Cloisters Apocalypse is also connected with Upper Rhenish painting as seen in the famous Manesse Codex.   JLS

Workshop of Jean Pucelle or Master of the Breviary of Charles V (?)
French (Paris), about 1345
Prayer book of Bonne of Luxembourg
  Manuscript on parchment, illuminated
  4 15/16 x 3½ in.
  The Cloisters Collection, 69.86

The suave, calligraphic style fostered by mid-fourteenth-century Parisian illuminators of luxury manuscripts is seen here in one of the most notable examples. The commission was realized for Bonne, Duchess of Normandy and wife of Duke Jean, later Jean II "le bon," King of France. The manuscript is remarkable for the miniatures of the Three Living and the Three Dead on facing pages, a grand concept for such a small manuscript and a poignant image of the temporal parallel to "dying in Christ." JLS

School of the Rimini Master
German (Middle Rhenish), 1420–1440
Mary Magdalen at the foot of the Cross
  Alabaster
  H. 8 7/16 in.
  Gift of Paul W. Doll, Jr., 65.85

This figure probably comes from a retable of the Crucifixion. Mary Magdalen is represented as an almost childish young woman, with an expression of quiet devotion, quite different from the dramatic and theatrical figure found so often in other schools. CG-M

Master of Cabestany
Spanish (Navarre), from the church of Errondo, near Unciti, 12th c.
Tympanum and Lintel: The three temptations of Christ, angels ministering to him, and the Lamb of God flanked by pairs of angels
  Limestone
  H. tympanum 31 in.
  The Cloisters Collection, 65.122.1,2

The subject of the tympanum illustrates Matthew IV:1–11. Related monuments in southern France and Italy are possibly by the same master. JLS

Enthroned Virgin and Child
  Austrian, probably Vienna, about 1360
  Lindenwood, polychromed and gilded
  H. 29⅝ in.
  The Cloisters Collection, 65.215.1

The stylistic parentage for this elegant and lissome seated group is in the fourteenth-century sculptures of the great Court School of Prague, yet the piece's particular charm is that of the School of Vienna. Additional figures probably completed a group representing the Adoration of the Magi. JLS

Master of the Altar of Rimini
  North French-Netherlandish, about 1420–1440
Kneeling angel, from an Annunciation group
  Alabaster
  H. 14½ in.
  The Cloisters Collection, 65.215.3

The finesse of carving and the intense realism of this piece, which shows the stylistic traits of the most important North French-Netherlandish sculptor of alabaster, far surpass his English counterparts at Nottingham in creativity and standard of execution. JLS

Bust of a lady of rank
  Byzantine, late 5th c.
  Marble
  H. 20⅞ in.
  The Cloisters Collection, 66.25

The woman, holding a scroll indicating her intellectual leanings, may originally have been accompanied by a portrait of her husband, attached to her at the right shoulder. The delicate carving of the face and headdress resembles that of the best imperial portraits of the time. MEF

Head of the Emperor Constans (?)
   Early Christian, about 340
   Marble
   H. 10⅜ in.
   Rogers Fund, 67.107

One of the finest portraits to survive from the Constantinian period, this head may represent the youngest son of Constantine I, Constans, who governed Italy, Africa, and Illyrium, 337–350.

MEF

Enthroned Virgin and Child
   French (Auvergne), second half of 12th c.
   Wood, polychromed
   H. 26¾ in.
   The Cloisters Collection, 67.153

From the same workshop and period, possibly even by the same hand, as an enthroned Virgin and Child given to the Museum by J. Pierpont Morgan in 1917, this sculpture is one of the finest Romanesque interpretations of the *Sedes Sapientiae*, or Throne of Wisdom, from Auvergne.

JLS

Angel of the Annunciation
   Italian, Venice, about 1425
   Istrian stone, painted and gilded
   H. 37¼ in.
   The Cloisters Collection, 67.236

One of the greatest masterpieces of Venetian sculpture of the fifteenth century, this was probably part of a monumental tomb. It is closely related in style and expression to two sculptures of the Madonna and Child in the church of San Marco.

CG-M

Gil de Siloe
   Spanish, School of Burgos, 1489–1493
Saint James the Greater
   Alabaster with touches of gold and polychrome
   H. 17¼ in.
   The Cloisters Collection, 69.88

From the royal tomb of Juan II and Isabel of Portugal in the Cartuja de Miraflores, Burgos. The monumentality, elegance, and exquisite carving are unquestionably the work of the master himself, who worked with assistants in other parts of the complicated tomb. Probably from the Netherlands, Siloe became completely integrated into the Spanish artistic activity of the period.

                                                                    CG-M

Tilman Riemenschneider and assistants
   German (Würzburg), about 1515–1520
Seated bishop
   Lindenwood
   H. 50 in.
   The Cloisters Collection, 1970.137.1

The manner of carving the deeply wrinkled face derives from an early work of Riemenschneider, the tomb of Rudolph von Scherenberg.   JLS

Saint Christopher carrying the Child Jesus
   Lower Rhenish, about 1470–1480
   Wood, polychromed and gilded
   H. 56 in.
   The Cloisters Collection, 1973.135

Before its recent purchase, this magnificent sculpture was the treasured guest of the Medieval Department for many years as a loan from Mrs. George Trubner. The eccentric form of the drapery and the mischievous rapport between the two figures create an unforgettable image of this popular saint.   CG-M

Tilman van der Burch and assistants
  German (Cologne and the Lower Rhine), end of
    15th c.
*Central shrine of an altarpiece: the Death of the
Virgin*
  Oak and elm
  H. 5 ft. 9 in.
  The Cloisters Collection, 1973.348

The figures perform like actors on a stage in this
highly realistic, but also expressionistic, representation, which employs the perspective devices
of fifteenth-century Netherlandish painters. The
illusion of depth is achieved in a moderately
shallow space through the perspective and a
combination of relief and semirelief carving.
Though the design concept and mechanical prin-
ciple are more sophisticated than the actual carving, this piece belongs among the most significant
examples of German sculpture of the time.   JLS

*Enthroned Virgin and Child with crowning and
musical angels*
  North Italian, Milan, early 15th c.
  Limestone relief
  H. 32¼ in.
  Bequest of Irwin Untermyer, 1974.126.4

The International style had a strong impact on
the artists working in and around the Cathedral
of Milan. This relief shows the beauty and eclec-
ticism of the style, particularly in the linear treatment of the drapery folds and the floating curls
of the angels' hair.   CG-M

Three exterior decorations from a secular building
  England (possibly London) or France (Calais),
    about 1500–1510
  Oak
  H. of each, approximately, before restoration,
    7 ft.
  The Cloisters Collection, 1974.295.1-3

In certain regions secular multistoried houses of
half-timber construction received extensive exterior decorations at the end of the Middle Ages.
These vigorously carved beam supports from
such a house were purchased as English, since the
arms of England quartered with those of France
appear on one of them. However, Calais belonged
to the English until the middle of the sixteenth
century, and it has been suggested that the carvings were made for a house in Calais by the
Franco-Flemish workshop of Georges Ambroise.
                                        JLS

Enthroned Virgin and Child
  Austrian, probably Linz, second quarter 13th c.
  Beechwood, with traces of polychromy
  H. 33 in.
  The Cloisters Collection, 1975.24

Although this transitional-style (from late Romanesque to early Gothic) sculpture probably originated in Austria, the ultimate origin of its style, and possibly also of its carver, is the Meuse Valley and the Rhineland. The Child's foot being caught and covered by the Virgin's drapery, a highly unusual iconographic feature, gives almost the effect that the Child is stepping out of His mother's womb.   JLS

Tilman Riemenschneider
  German (Würzburg), about 1505
Standing bishop, probably Saint Valentine
  Lindenwood, polychromed and gilded
  H. 46⅛ in.
  The Cloisters Collection, 1975.25

Riemenschneider's mastery of the technical means of achieving Late Gothic realism comes through as much in this sculpture as does his consummate skill in creating interest and balancing line and mass. The figure probably stands chronologically between his large Saint James the Greater in Munich and his Saint Matthias in Berlin-Dahlem. All three served as prototypes for stone figures of apostles executed by Riemenschneider and his workshop for the exterior of the Marienkapelle in Würzburg.   JLS

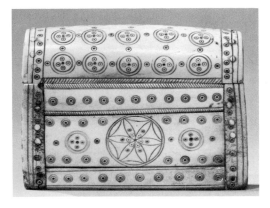

Reliquary casket
  North Italian or German, 10th–11th c.
  Bone
  H. 2⅜ in.
  Rogers Fund, 65.68.2

The incised circle motif, initially a form of decoration on Coptic ivories and employed especially on utilitarian objects, was widely used in Europe in the early Middle Ages. A casket this small may have been carried around the neck as a purse reliquary.   CTL

Plaque: Christ on the road to Emmaus and the Supper of Emmaus
    French, Carolingian, School of Metz, about 870
    Ivory
    H. 4 17/32 in.
    The Cloisters Collection, 1970.324.1

Created by one of the most gifted carvers at Metz for one of the long sides of a casket, this is one of the few accurate reflections of a Carolingian cycle of New Testament illustration. All contemporary manuscript evidence of this has been lost.
                                                    JLS

Plaque: Saint Demetrius of Saloniki
    Byzantine, about 1000
    Ivory
    H. 7¾ in.
    The Cloisters Collection, 1970.324.3

This powerful and striking image, in battle dress of the imperial late antique period, may have had a companion piece (Saint George is the saint who most often accompanies Demetrius) or may have been set into a casket with other plaques.   JLS

Piece from a game of draughts: Hercules slaying Geryon
    German (Cologne), about 1130
    Ivory
    D. 2¾ in.
    The Cloisters Collection, 1970.324.4

Mythological heroes, popular subjects in the Middle Ages, made their way to the gaming table in this set of pieces, of which we have one. JLS

Pyxis
Hispano-Moresque, about 950–975
Ivory
H. 4½ in.
The Cloisters Collection, 1970.324.5

Lions, gazelles, and parrots in pairs, surrounded by richly carved vine scroll decoration, arranged in strict symmetry, ornament this cylindrical container, one of the most accomplished works attributed to a master from Madinat az-Zahra, the palace of Caliph Abderrahman III (912–961).
JLS

Diptych: the Last Judgment and the Coronation of the Virgin
French (Paris), end of 13th c.
Ivory
H. 4⅞ in.
The Cloisters Collection, 1970.324.7a,b

Masterful composition, subtle detail, and deep carving make this one of the most original and penetrating miniature sculptures of the Parisian high court style.
JLS

Plaque: the murder of Thomas à Becket
English, about 1400
Ivory
H. 3½ in.
The Cloisters Collection, 1970.324.10

The ajouré technique and crowded composition, in which spindly architectural forms lose all sense of true function and stability, characterize a group of English International-style ivory carvings that have been unjustly publicized as nineteenth-century forgeries.
JLS

Diptych: the Virgin and Child with candle-bearing angels, and Crucifixion
  French or German (Cologne?) third quarter of 14th c.
  Ivory
  H. 6½ in.
  The Cloisters Collection, 1971.49.3a,b

This excellently carved work with its heavy forms seems more French-inspired than typically Ile-de-France in workmanship.   JLS

Plaque: the Tree of Jesse
  German (Franconia, Bamberg[?]), early 13th c.
  Ivory
  H. 3⅜ in.
  Purchased jointly by The Metropolitan Museum of Art (The Cloisters Collection) and the Réunion des Musées Nationaux de France (Palais du Louvre), 1973.70

The hieratic attitude of the Virgin, supporting the Christ Child over her head, sets this representation iconographically apart from all other known examples of the theme. The inclusion of Bishop Fulbert (right), the eleventh-century bishop of Chartres, as a counterpart to the prophet Isaiah (left) is in itself exceedingly rare and is limited to late Romanesque and early Gothic German usage. Perhaps intended to decorate a book cover or a casket, the plaque is carved from the material saved from an ivory comb.

                                      JLS

Plaque: the Crucifixion and the Three Marys at the Tomb
  Carolingian (Metz School), about 870
  Ivory
  H. 9 in.
  Purchased jointly by The Metropolitan Museum of Art (The Cloisters Collection) and the Réunion des Musées Nationaux de France (Palais du Louvre), 1974.266

This originally decorated the front cover of a liturgical manuscript. The artist altered a standard Metz School composition in order to include the scene of the Three Marys at the tomb.   JLS

Plaque: the Annunciation
　Austrian (Klosterneuburg), 15th c. (?)
　Champlevé and cloisonné enamel on copper-
　　gilt.
　8⅛ x 6½ in.
　The Cloisters Collection, 65.3

Under the impact of his model, the Annunciation
plaque on the Altar of Klosterneuburg by Nicholas of Verdun, the artist has so cleverly concealed
the stylistic tendencies of his own generation that
the precise date of the plaque has eluded all who
have studied it. This imitator—or early
"forger"—maintains artistic independence and
late Gothic character while translating the late
twelfth-century style and composition and employs the rare medieval technique of granite
enamel for the lectern.   JLS

*Rosary pendant: the Virgin and Child in Glory
on the crescent moon*
　German, early 16th c.
　Silver, partly gilded
　D. 2 5/16 in.
　The Cloisters Collection, 65.68.1

The late medieval goldsmith could maintain high
quality of workmanship while "mass-producing"
objects after a single model, as this one and an
almost identical example in the Kunsthistorisches
Museum in Vienna demonstrate.   JLS

Silver spoon
　Syria, 5th–6th c.
　L. 9 1/16 in.
　Rogers Fund, 65.87

Richly decorated with incised and nielloed leaf
patterns and Christian symbols. One of the more
elaborate spoons to have survived from this
period, it may have been used during the mass
in an Early Christian church or, as has sometimes
been suggested for similar spoons, as a gift on the
occasion of its owner's baptism.   MEF

Plaque: the Pentecost
  Mosan, third quarter of 12th c.
  Champlevé enamel on copper-gilt.
  4 1/16 x 4 1/16 in.
  The Cloisters Collection, 65.105

Three companion plaques, gifts of J. Pierpont
Morgan in 1917, were in the Museum's collection
when this one was purchased. All represent
scenes from the Life and Passion of Christ and
stylistically recall the work of Godefroid de
Claire, the master enamelist of the Meuse Valley
around 1160. One can easily imagine the original
resplendent object, possibly a portable altar,
originally decorated by these plaques, notable for
the brilliance of their enamel and the strong
classical element in their style.   JLS

Tabernacle with folding wings
  Austrian (Salzburg), 1494
  Silver parcel-gilt, enamel, and mother-of-pearl
  H. 27 3/8 in.
  Gift of Mr. and Mrs. Leopold Blumka, 69.226

A rare object with a complete pedigree, this was
made by Perchtold (Pertoldus aurofaber) for
Rupert, abbot of the Benedictine monastery in
Salzburg. Inscriptions on the piece and documents in the monastery confirm this. The scene
of the Last Supper on the back is taken from an
engraving by Master I. A. M. Zwolle. One of the
most important gifts received by the Medieval
Department, it was given in commemoration of
the centennial of the Museum.   CG-M

Fragment of a woman's girdle
  South German, early 16th c.
  Silver-gilt
  L. 28½ in.
  The Cloisters Collection, 1972.138

Ten elements of metal openwork in the "wood
shaving" pattern popular about 1500, with a
rosette in the center of each rectangle, make up
the length of the girdle (incomplete). Small ban-
derolles between the links bear engraved Latin
words and initials making up an inscription that
can no longer be deciphered.   JLS

Crib of the Infant Jesus
   South Netherlandish (Brabant), mid-15th c.
   Carved and polychromed wood, lead, silver-gilt, painted parchment, and silk embroidered with seed pearls, gold thread, tinsel, and translucent enamels
   12½ x 11 x 7 3/16 in.
   Gift of Ruth Blumka in memory of Leopold Blumka, 1974.121

This richest and most elaborate of several such cribs, known as "Repos de Jésus," comes from the Grand Béguinage of Louvain. It is thought that the cribs were given to young novices when they took their vows.   CG-M

Châsse with the Annunciation, Visitation, Nativity, Annunciation to the Shepherds, Crucifixion, Resurrection, and Peter and Paul
   French (Limoges [?]), third quarter of 13th c.
   Copper-gilt and champlevé enamel, crystal finials and semiprecious stones, cabochons, on a wooden core
   13½ x 13½ x 5 in.
   Bequest of Harriet H. Jonas, 1974.288.1

One of a small group known as *châsses à transept* because of their architectural shape. Typical of the group are the appliqué figures with enameled costumes and expressive faces, the use of decorative cabochons, the sketchy style of the representations on the back, and, for Limoges pieces, the unusual iconography exemplified here in the representation of the resurrected Christ as a beardless youth.   CG-M

Pendant: Saint Michael slaying the dragon
   French, about 1470–1480
   Mother-of-pearl, polychromy and gilding, (partly renewed) with silver mounting of the 16th c.
   H. 2 1/16 in.
   The Cloisters Collection, 1975.65

The earliest known badge for the knightly order of St. Michael, founded at Amboise by Louis XI in 1469. *Immensi tremor oceani* ("terror of the immense ocean"), the motto of the order, explains the use of mother-of-pearl rather than some more precious material.   JLS

Oil jar in the shape of a bear
 Late Roman–Early Christian, 3rd–4th c.
 Bronze
 H. 5⅜ in.
 Edith Perry Chapman Fund, 66.18

One of the finest of a group of such jars, made from the second to sixth centuries. The bear was a popular animal in the circus games and in itinerant shows. Probably a secular object, this jar could have belonged to a pagan as well as to a Christian household. MEF

Pilgrim's flask
 Byzantine, 6th–8th c.
 Copper
 H. 4 7/16 in.
 Rogers Fund, 67.200.2

Rare in material and in shape. Judging from the stamped images of an equestrian saint on the neck band, it must have come from an important church of a military saint, perhaps in Asia Minor, perhaps in Thessaloniki—where it might have been produced for the shrine and basilica of Saint Demetrius. MEF

Attributed to Aert van Tricht the Elder
 South Netherlandish (Maastricht), about 1500
Eagle Lectern
 Brass, cast and chased
 H. 6 ft. 7½ in.
 The Cloisters Collection, 68.8

Traditionally, and no doubt correctly, this elaborate and monumental lectern is said to have originally adorned the north (epistle) side of the high altar of the Collegiate Church of Saint Peter in Louvain, for which it must have been made. The smaller figures include the Virgin and Child, Christ, the Three Magi, saints, and prophets.

JLS

Covered jug
North German or Netherlandish, 14th c.
Bronze
H. 17⅛ in.
The Cloisters Collection, 1972.141

On the lid is a molded and incised representation of a human head. Such jugs probably carried hot and cold water in the late medieval household. A jug of identical size in the Irwin Untermyer Collection (64.101.1527) may have been cast in the same mold, though its top is undecorated.   JLS

Chandelier
Early Christian, 6th–7th c.
Bronze and brass
H. 13 11/16 in.
The Cloisters Collection, 1974.150

The globe with foliate branches for lights and the hand holding a cross on an orb were probably not originally intended to go together. While rare in form, the globe with lights, adhering to a Late Antique tradition of branched chandeliers, resembles a hanging lamp portrayed in the mosaics of St. George at Thessaloniki. The hand with cross, which is decorated with incised figures of the Virgin and Christ Child and Saints Peter, Paul, Stephen, Cosmas, and Damian, is the most elaborate of a number of similar pieces that have survived from the early centuries of our era. The prayer to Christ and the invocation of Saints Cosmas and Damian as well as the form of the hand recall the apotropaic hands of the god Sabazios, whose mystery cult was popular in the Late Roman period.   MEF

Three windows: scenes from the lives of Christ, the Virgin, and saints
Austrian, Church of Saint Leonhard, Lavant-thal, about 1340
Stained glass
H. each window 15 ft. 11 in.
The Cloisters Collection, 65.96.1-4, 65.97.1-6, 65.98, 68.224.1 (illustrated)–13, 1970.320

The most important recent acquisitions of medieval stained glass by the Museum, these panels came from several sources. The first group was bought at auction in London, the Appearances window was acquired by purchase and exchange with the Virginia Museum of Fine Arts, and the final piece was purchased at a sale in Lucerne. Consisting of two complete windows, one with its original tracery lights, and parts from three others, this glass constitutes the most extensive collection of Austrian stained glass from a single church in a foreign country.   JH

Two Apostles
  French, Rouen, second quarter of 14th c.
  Stained glass, grisaille paint with silver stain
  10¼ x 8½ in.
  The Cloisters Collection, 69.236.1

Unlike most medieval stained glass, which was bound by hieratical religious concepts, these figures possess a charm and verve indicative of the personality of the artist. It is thought that manuscript illuminators like Jean Pucelle inspired this type of canopy figure.   JH

Saint Martin dividing his cloak with the beggar
  German, Rhenish, 15th c.
  Stained glass, grisaille paint with silver stain
  D. 7⅞ in.
  The Cloisters Collection, 1971.278

Engravings, widely circulated in the latter part of the fifteenth century, frequently served as models for roundels of stained glass made for the windows of private houses or civil buildings. This is an early example of the influence of printmaking.   JH

Sleeping monk, woman distributing alms
  French, Paris, Abbey of Saint Germain-des-
    Pres, about 1245
  Stained glass
  H. 25¼ in.
  The Cloisters Collection, 1973.262.1,2

Made for the Lady Chapel of the abbey, these panels come from a window depicting the history of the building of the abbey, the royal donations that made it possible, and the activities of the monastic community.   JH

Tapestry: Madonna and Child with Saint Anne and Saint Joseph
 Flemish, Brussels, about 1500
 Wool and metal thread
 48½ x 53⅞ in.
 Bequest of Adele L. Lehman in memory of Arthur Lehman, 65.181.15

In size and subject matter this resembles a painting, the frame contributing to this effect. Originally at the Cathedral of Burgos, this precious tapestry was probably acquired under royal patronage. CG-M

Tapestry: the story of Perseus and Andromeda
 Flemish, Brussels, about 1510–1520
 Wool and silk
 11 ft. 2 in. x 11 ft.
 Bequest of Adele L. Lehman in memory of Arthur Lehman, 65.181.16

Typical of the complicated Brussels tapestries of the time, this represents Andromeda's parents imploring Perseus to save their daughter. In the background she is shown tied to the rock, and the hero is fighting the dragon. Perhaps from a set of eight tapestries—of which two others are known—bought by Emperor Charles V from the manufacturer and dealer Gabriel van der Tommen in 1521. CG-M

Tapestry: five boys playing "hoodman blind"
 French, Touraine
 Silk and wool
 8 ft. 10 in. x 10 ft. 5 in.
 Bequest of Adele L. Lehman in memory of Arthur Lehman, 65.181.17

The inscription reads *selon le temps* ("according to the times" or "there is a time for everything, even play"). The meaning of the cipher DG in the lower corners is unknown. CG-M

Tapestries: *le Cerf Fragile*
  Franco-Flemish, about 1520
  Wool and silk
  38¼ x 34¼ in.
  Bequest of Adele L. Lehman in memory of
    Arthur Lehman, 65.181.18–22

This set of five portrays the Cerf (human life) chased first by Nature and Youth, then by Vanity and Ignorance, followed by Old Age, and finally Sickness with Death in the background. The poet in his epilogue speaks of the perishability of terrestrial life and the hope in God. The set has an intimacy and directness seldom conveyed by large tapestries.   CG-M

Hanging: *scenes from the Old and New Testaments*
  German (Lower Saxony, probably vicinity of
    Hildesheim), late 14th c.
  Linen embroidered with silk, faces and inscriptions painted
  60⅝ x 61 7/16 in.
  The Cloisters Collection, Gift of Mrs. W.
    Murray Crane and Louise Crane, 69.106

An illuminated manuscript probably served as the pattern book for this, one of two fragments known of a hanging meant to be displayed over choir stalls or around the apse of a church interior. The work was done by nuns in a convent, and the emphasis is on the complicated and colorful needlework rather than on artistic exegesis.   JLS

Tapestry: *two riddles of the Queen of Sheba*
  Germany, Alsatian (Strasbourg [?]), last quarter
    of 15th c.
  Wool, silk, gold, and silver threads
  31½ x 40 in.
  The Cloisters Collection, 1971.43

Few medieval tapestries with the Ghiordes knot, a Turkish rug-pile technique, survive. Here the knot simulates the velvet costumes. This is the earliest representation in tapestry or textile of the legend of the Queen of Sheba riddling King Solomon about the genders of children and the difference between natural and artificial roses.   JLS

Tapestry: the Annunciation
 Flemish (Tournai[?]) or French, about 1460–1470
 Wool and silk
 42½ x 83¾ in.
 The Cloisters Collection, 1971.135

The unusual combination of exterior and interior settings adds to the considerable iconographic interest and points to the composition's source in Netherlandish paintings. Otherwise, the forms in painted prototypes have been taken over almost exclusively for their decorative value.   JLS

Praetexta of an Antependium
 Rhenish, School of Cologne, after 1450
 Linen embroidered and woven with silk and
  gold thread
 L. 77¾ in.
 Gift of Alastair Bradley Martin, 1973.312

Narrow bands like this were placed on top of an altar frontal to cover the edge of the altar. All the saints represented here—Bridget, Martin, Benedict, and Servatius—were associated with the Rhine valley near Cologne.   CG-M

Tapestry: five figures on a millefleurs background
 French, probably Tournai, early 16th c.
 Wool
 Bequest of Harriet H. Jonas, 1974.228.2

The gentleman in the middle holding a falcon seems to be taking leave of his lady, while his attendants and the hound wait to begin the hunt. Tapestries with figures floating, as here, on "verdure" backgrounds seem to have been produced in France rather than the Netherlands.   CG-M

Plate decorated with deer and hares
 Byzantine, 12th c.
 Glazed terracotta
 D. 8¾ in.
 Anonymous Gift and Rogers Fund, 1971.147.2

A survivor of the enormous production of table-
ware in the Byzantine empire, the decoration
derives ultimately from antique prototypes, but
more immediately from tenth- and eleventh-
century secular images of the hunt. The anatomical confusions are typical of a design so often
copied that it has little reference to natural forms.

MEF

Sho
 Early Tokugawa period (1615–1867), Japan
 L. 17⅞ in.
 Rogers Fund, 68.62.2

Above the lacquered wind reservoir, decorated with two phoenixes, seventeen free-reed pipes are arranged in a traditional form that symbolizes the phoenix. The metal reeds produce soft chords when the player blows into, or draws air from, the short neck.

Guitar
 18th c., Italy
 L. 36 in.
 Rogers Fund, 69.29

The back of this fine six-string guitar is profusely inlaid with ivory and ebony ornaments; the fingerboard is covered with tortoise shell, and the rosette, carved of dark ivory, is surrounded by an especially ornate hexagonal band of marguerites and musical motifs.

Pipe organ
 About 1835, eastern United States
 By William Crowell
 H. 81 in.
 Rogers Fund, 1974.193

No other instruments from Crowell's hands survive, yet the casework and three ranks of wood pipes show the touch of an experienced organ builder. This chamber instrument is pumped with one pedal, another operates the swell shutters, and there are six hand stops at the sides of the single keyboard.

Violin
  1662, Cremona, Italy
  By Nicolò Amati
  L. 23¼ in.
  Gift of Evelyn Stark, 1974.229a–d

Nicolò was the greatest artist-craftsman of the Amati family; both Andrea Guarneri and Antonio Stradivari are said to have been trained in his workshop. This violin was once owned by Paul Julien, when it was awarded to him as first-prize winner at the National Conservatory of Music in Lucerne.

Steel drums
  1974, New York
  By Vincent Taylor
  D. each drum 22½ in.
  Gift of Vincent Taylor, 1974.114a–e

Steel drums (or "piano pans"), hammered by hand from heat-treated steel oil-drums, are among the most important and popular Latin American instruments. This set, made by a Trinidadian craftsman who is also a virtuoso performer, represents a recent stage in the development of an instrument family that has ancestors in the prehistoric Orient.

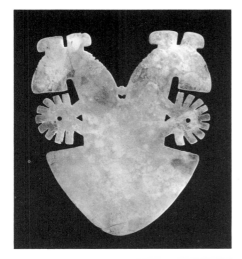

Pendant
    Date uncertain, Tolima (Colombia)
    Gold
    H. 6¼ in.
    Jointly owned by Mrs. Harold L. Bache and The
      Metropolitan Museum of Art, 66.196.18

Tolima goldwork is perhaps the most formally stylized of all the many Precolumbian productions. Often virtually abstract in design, it is particularly appealing to the modern eye.

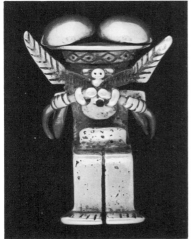

Pendant: animal-headed figure
    Date uncertain, Quimbaya (Colombia)
    Gold
    H. 2½ in.
    Jointly owned by Mrs. Harold L. Bache and The
      Metropolitan Museum of Art, 66.196.20

A consistently used figure in the gold of ancient Colombia is this one, with human body, animal-snout head, leaflike "ears," and headdress topped with two domed elements. Its significance is unknown. Such figures, varying considerably in style, have been found as far afield as the Parita area of Panama.

Pendant: figures with "bat" attributes
    1100–1500, Parita (Azuero peninsula, Panama)
    Gold
    H. 3⅛ in.
    Jointly owned by Mrs. Harold L. Bache and The
      Metropolitan Museum of Art, 66.196.34

Human figures with facial features often interpreted as those of bats—due primarily to the large, upturned noses—are of considerable iconographical importance in ancient Central America. These hold bundled staffs and paddle-shaped "standards," the missing portions of which were possibly made of shell or ivory.

Pair of ear spools
   A.D. 200–500, Mochica (Peru)
   Gold, stone, shell inlay
   D. 4 in.
   Jointly owned by Mrs. Harold L. Bache and The
      Metropolitan Museum of Art, 66.196.40,41

Such ornaments, imposing in size and rich in color, are among the great treasures of ancient Peruvian art. Bird-headed messengers dash across the face of these, clutching in outstretched hands their all-important small bags.

Pendant: figure with headdress
   1200–1500, Tairona (Sierra Nevada area, Colombia)
   Gold
   H. 5½ in.
   Gift of the H. L. Bache Foundation, 69.7.10

The small, pugnacious figures that appear as pendants among the Tairona are most extraordinary when the figures wear enormous headdresses that intricately combine bird and animal heads and multiple spiral elements. This figure, particularly elaborate, wears a lip plug in its lower lip and both ear and nose ornaments.

Funerary mask
   1200–1400, Chimu (Peru)
   Gold, overlays, paint
   H. 12¼ in.
   Jointly owned by Mrs. Harold L. Bache and The
      Metropolitan Museum of Art, 1974.271.35

Such masks were elaborately painted and ornamented. Almost the entire surface would be hidden, with perhaps only the nose and the outline of the eyes remaining uncovered.

Bell: effigy head
  Late 15th C., Mixtec (Valley of Oaxaca, Mexico)
  Gold
  H. 1 in.
  Jointly owned by Mrs. Harold L. Bache and The
    Metropolitan Museum of Art, 1974.271.49

Made as a bell, this still retains its original
clapper. The large opening through the nose is
presumed to have held some form of dangling
ornament; such ornaments are often large enough
to cover the mouth.

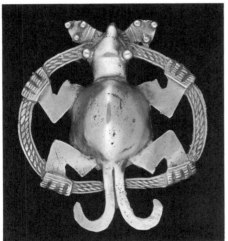

Bell pendant: turtle with snakes
  A.D. 800–1200, Veraguas (Panama)
  Gold
  H. 4 in.
  Jointly owned by Mrs. Harold L. Bache and The
    Metropolitan Museum of Art, 1974.271.50

The body forms a bell; two snakes encircle the
turtle and are firmly held by it. Turtles and frogs
are frequent in the goldwork of the Precolumbian
Americas, but the ancient meanings of these representations are unclear.

Ornament: stylized bird
  A.D. 600–1000, Coastal Huari-Tiahuanaco (Peru)
  Gold
  H. 6½ in.
  Jointly owned by Mrs. Harold L. Bache and The
    Metropolitan Museum of Art, 1974.271.54

Gold objects of Huari-Tiahuanaco style are rare
and documentation on them is scant. This bird,
which has profile heads on the end of its wings
and frontal faces at the end of its tail, probably
comes from the Central Coast rather than from
the highland sites of Huari and Tiahuanaco.

Stirrup spout vessel: crouching figure
  700–400 B.C., late Chavin (Jequetepeque valley,
    Peru)
  Burnished redware, red pigment
  H. 10⅝ in.
  Harris Brisbane Dick Fund, 67.239.5

The art of Chavin is the earliest important work known from ancient Peru, and in spite of its early date it exhibits the most complex iconographic system ever devised in Precolumbian South America. The crouching figure on this vessel, apparently emerging from a shell, is an uncommon Chavin image.

Stirrup spout vessel: fruit (?)
  700–400 B.C., late Chavin (Jequetepeque valley,
    Peru)
  Burnished redware, pigment
  H. 10 5/16 in.
  Harris Brisbane Dick Fund, 67.239.7

Vessels of sculptural form with constricted, spouted openings were a much favored pottery form in ancient Peru. The stirrup spout was consistently used throughout some three thousand years of Peruvian prehistory.

Yoke-form vessel
  About A.D. 500, Maya (Mexico or Guatemala)
  Variegated blackware
  H. 11 in.
  Purchase, Mrs. Charles S. Payson Gift, 1970.138

Maya pottery vessels of the fifth to sixth centuries are among the most singularly inventive ceramic productions in all of ancient Maya art. This vessel, the iconographic associations of which relate to the ritual ball game, is a unique combination of a yoke form and lidded cylinder.

Pair of storage jars
   300–100 B.C., late Paracas (Palpa valley, Peru)
   Grayware, postfired paint
   H. 18½ in.
   Gift of Nathan Cummings, 1974.123.1,2

The incised and painted design on the upper third of these large jars is principally one of fantastic figures with attached trophy heads. Open-winged falcons appear also, the raised heads of which form nubbins; the falcon heads face in a different direction on each jar.

Mask
   Bamileke, Bagam group, eastern Grasslands, Cameroon
   Wood, kaolin
   H. 28 in.
   Louis V. Bell Fund, 1971.13

Unusual in style, this combines rather spare features with the bulging cheeks commonly found in Grasslands art.

Diviner's bowl
  Yoruba, southwestern Nigeria
  Wood, beads
  H. 9 in.
  Rogers Fund, 1971.91

The mother and child that support the bowl serve no ritual function but represent an ultimate good in Yoruba thinking, something greatly desired by most of the diviner's clients.

Mask
  Kom, western Grasslands, Cameroon
  Wood
  H. 27 in.
  Fletcher Fund, 1971.4.2

Small heads and spears top the principal face. This and similar masks may have belonged to the Ngumba regulatory society, an agency of traditional government.

Mask
  Fungom, Bamenda Highlands, Cameroon
  Wood, paint
  H. 13¼ in.
  Fletcher Fund, 1972.4.5

Worn during an annual dance by the ruler's retainers. A bundle of colored feathers would have filled the opening on the crown.

Mask
Widekum, Maghamo group, western Cameroon
Wood, paint
H. 22 in.
Fletcher Fund, 1972.4.12

Information collected with the mask indicates that it was carved in the nineteenth century and used by an association of hunters. Represents no single animal but combines features of the ram and buffalo with a human nose.

Ancestral figure
Mambila, Saa group, northern Cameroon
Pith, paint
H. 14 1/16 in.
Fletcher Fund, 1972.4.15

These fragile little figures were placed in ancestral shrines, palm-wine groves, and other places where their magical powers warded off intruders.

Stool
Duala, coastal Cameroon
Wood
H. 11¼ in.
Fletcher Fund, 1972.4.31

Collected by a missionary in 1899, this is one of the rare examples of Duala art in the United States. Trading and missionary activities on the coast brought an end to traditional carving soon after 1900.

Stool
  Mambila, Bang group, northern Cameroon
  Wood, paint
  H. 12 in.
  Fletcher Fund, 1972.4.32

Purchased in 1934 by Paul Gebauer, who reports that it was used in circumcision rites by the rulers of Bang until 1925, when the chief was converted to Islam and abandoned the practice.

Tobacco pipe bowl
  Bamileke, Bagam group, eastern Grasslands, Cameroon
  Bronze
  H. 5¼ in.
  Fletcher Fund, 1972.4.41

Cast by the lost-wax process, bronze pipes were relatively rare in traditional Grasslands society; their use indicated high status.

Artist's model pipe bowl
  Bamessing, Nsei group, western Grasslands, Cameroon
  Terracotta
  H. 3⅞ in.
  Fletcher Fund, 1972.4.46

Models of successful pipe designs were kept in the workshop for apprentices to study and copy.

Artist's model pipe bowl
  Bamessing, Nsei group, western Grasslands,
    Cameroon
  Terracotta
  H. 3½ in.
  Fletcher Fund, 1972.4.48

This style of bowl, seldom seen today, had fallen out of fashion by 1936 when Paul Gebauer acquired this model in the Bamessing market.

War knife
  Kaka, Kwadja group, northern Cameroon
  Iron, wood
  H. 20¼ in.
  Fletcher Fund, 1972.4.64

The form of the knife and the chasing on the blade far exceed the requirements of utility. Carried by men in ceremonial war dances.

Saltcellar
  Early 16th c., Bini-Portuguese
  Ivory
  H. 7 in.
  Louis V. Bell and Rogers Funds, 1972.63

Discovered in Europe but carved in Africa to Portuguese specifications. The style is clearly related to Benin court ivories. Double-chambered and made in three parts; the hemispherical lid is missing.

Tomb figure
  Bongo, Republic of Sudan
  Wood
  H. 75½ in.
  Louis V. Bell and Harris Brisbane Dick Funds,
    Joseph Pulitzer Bequest, 1973.264

Near the graves of important men stood sculptures representing the deceased, his wives, and
children. This example was meant to be seen with
the post sunk in the earth.

Rattle staff (uxure)
  1735–1750, court of Benin, Nigeria
  Bronze
  H. 64 in.
  Anne and George Blumenthal Fund, 1974.5

The *oba* (king) holds a stone celt and an *uxure*
and stands on an elephant flanked by leopards.
Executioners' knives and swords of authority are
on the shaft. At the bottom: another elephant, an
alligator, snakes, human figures, and other motifs.

Model for brass cast
  Baule, Ivory Coast
  Wax
  H. 8½ in.
  Gift of Ernst Anspach, 1974.387

This model, in a recent style, was meant to be
cast by lost wax, a technique known in Black
Africa since at least A.D. 800.

Breastplate for an Esu devotee
  Yoruba, Nigeria
  Wood, leather, shells, metal, ivory, beads
  H. 30 in.
  Gift of Mr. and Mrs. Joseph Gerofsky, 1974.388.1

Little is known about objects of this type, though they seem to have been worn during festivals in honor of Esu the trickster. The leather cord passed around the neck, the cowrie shells hung down the breast.

Prints and Photographs

Comments by Janet S. Byrne, Curator, Colta Feller Ives and Mary L. Myers, Associate Curators, Weston J. Naef, Assistant Curator, and Suzanne Boorsch and David W. Kiehl, Curatorial Assistants

---

Herwig
　18th c., German

Silhouette Portrait of a Lady
　Cut and painted, mounted on embossed paper
　　by Reder
　8¾ x 5½ in.
　Mary Martin Fund, 65.552

Silhouettes as attractive and interesting as this one, a delightful addition to our large silhouette collection, seldom change ownership.

Michael Burghers
　Active in England 1676–1720, Netherlandish

Frontispiece to Book I of Paradise Lost, *4th ed., London, 1688*
　Engraving
　11¼ x 7½ in.
　The Elisha Whittelsey Collection, the Elisha
　　Whittelsey Fund, 66.558.1

A great text often overwhelms an illustrator. The very first illustrations for *Paradise Lost,* published in its fourth edition, were on the whole weak, but this splendid engraving stands out in its bold, classic strength.

Charles Meryon
1821–1866, French

Le Pont au Change
Etching, proof between states 6 and 7
Pencil corrections and additions in the artist's
hand
6⅛ x 13 in.
Bequest of Susan Dwight Bliss, 67.630.9

Devoted to Paris's old buildings and bridges,
Meryon etched them in copper to assure their
preservation, adding, in the process, fantastic vi-
sions of chariots, serpents, and goddesses reclining in the clouds.

Karl Friedrich Schinkel
1781–1841, German

Plate V, Möbel—Entwürfe
Lithograph, plate colored, 1835–1837
18¾ x 25 in.
Fletcher Fund, 67.735.291

As the chief architect of the Prussian princes
Schinkel was responsible for much of the neoclassical grandeur of Berlin. The furniture designs
he provided for one of the royal palaces were
published as a set of portfolios. The dependence
on gold leaf and classical design elements were
important characteristics of much of the interior
decoration of this period.

Francesco Piranesi
1758/59–1810, Italian

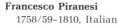

Illumination of the Cross in St. Peter's
Etching, hand colored with brown and gray
wash and white gouache
27 x 18½ in.
The Elisha Whittelsey Collection, the Elisha
Whittelsey Fund, 67.761.2

An unrecorded etching from a series designed by
a Frenchman, Louis Jean Desprez (1743–1804),
recording events of Holy Week in Rome. Desprez
was probably the one who added the colored
washes to the etching.

Erté (Romain de Tirtoff)
Born (in Russia) 1892, French

"L'Eté," costume design for "Mah-Jongg", Act II Scene I, George White's Scandals, *New York, 1924*
Gouache and metallic paint, signed
14⅞ x 10⅜ in.
Purchase, Gift of Jane Martin Ginsburg, President of the Martin Foundation, 67.762.120

L'Eté is one of fifteen Erté drawings for this scene and, along with a set, a curtain, and twelve other costume designs, forms a twentieth-century segment of the museum's theater collection.

Jean Viset
Working 1536, French

Six nude men, from a set of Gymnastic Figures
Etching, monogramed at lower left
10⅝ x 8 in.
The Elisha Whittelsey Collection, the Elisha Whittelsey Fund, 68.537

Little is known about Viset except that he worked in Fontainebleau. The monogram in the lower left corner has been interpreted as all of the letters of his name, but it also spells out the name of Juste de Juste (1505–1559), who also worked at Fontainebleau.

Edgar Degas
1834–1917, French

The Fireside (Le Foyer)
Monotype, 1880–1890
16 5/16 x 23⅛ in.
Harris Brisbane Dick Fund, The Elisha Whittelsey Collection, the Elisha Whittelsey Fund, and C. Douglas Dillon Gift, 68.670

Unjustly neglected until recently, Degas's more than 300 monotypes testify to his unorthodox vision and technique. One of the largest and most powerful of these "printed drawings," *The Fireside* depicts prostitutes in a brothel, and conveys the heavy, brooding atmosphere of the *maisons closes*.

Stefano della Bella
1610–1664, Italian

Death on the Battlefield
Etching, touched proof, 1646/47
7⅝ x 11⅝ in.
Harris Brisbane Dick Fund, The Elisha Whittelsey Collection, the Elisha Whittelsey Fund, by exchange, 68.736.1

Incomplete states of prints are rare, and such states with the artist's next thoughts sketched in are rarer still. Here the printed image is compelling already; the presence of della Bella's sketched-in figures at a point where he stopped to see how the print would look adds to its fascination.

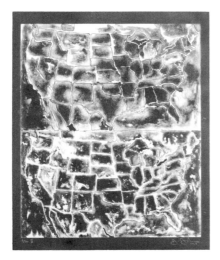

Jasper Johns
Born 1930, American

Two Maps II
Lithograph, signed and dated 1966; numbered 2/30 II
25¼ x 20¼ in.
Gift of Dr. Joseph I. Singer, Florence and Joseph I. Singer Collection, 68.749

A virtuoso printmaker, Johns has created in *Two Maps II* (the Roman numeral denotes the state) a totally different effect from *Two Maps I*, which was printed from the same stone but in white on black paper, and with an aluminum plate added; here the printing is in black on white semitransparent paper laid down on black paper, giving the lithograph a subtly rich and luminous quality.

Albrecht Dürer
1471–1528, German

Christ on the Mount of Olives
Etching
8¾ x 6⅛ in.
Gift of Mrs. George Khuner, the George Khuner Collection, 68.793.1

A gift of 127 Dürer prints included this sparkling impression of one of the artist's six etchings. Dürer had begun etching only in 1514, the year before this image was made, but already he showed mastery of the animated line and chiaroscuro effects possible with the technique.

Thomas Frye
1710–1762, English

Charlotte Sophia of Mecklenburg-Strelitz, Queen of George III
Mezzotint, proof before letters, 1762
24⅜ x 16⅞ in.
The Elisha Whittelsey Collection, the Elisha Whittelsey Fund, by exchange, 69.669.1

A proof state in exceptional condition; mezzotints are among the most fragile of the print mediums.

Melchior Meier
Active in Switzerland 1577–1582, German (?)

Saint William with Standard and Shield
Engraving
10⅞ x 7¾ in.
Rogers Fund, 1970.517.1

Hardly anything is known about the man who made this very rare engraving, to whom only a handful of prints have been attributed. He was in Freiburg, Switzerland, when he engraved and published this print, as the inscription states. It is tempting to think that at some time he worked as an armorer, for every plate and nail and all the handsome engraved ornament of the knightly saint's armor is shown in loving detail.

Henri de Toulouse-Lautrec
1864–1901, French

Miss Loie Fuller
Color lithograph with gilt, 1893
15 x 10 in.
Rogers Fund, 1970.534

Loie Fuller's "fire dance" was a spectacular hit at the Folies Bergère. To recreate its brilliant effect, Lautrec devised a billowy cloud to represent Loie's twirling skirts, then applied gold to each of the fifty lithographs he printed to capture the stage effects of smoke and light.

Richard Doyle
1824–1883, English

"The Fairy Queen takes an airy drive in a light carriage, a twelve-in-hand, drawn by thoroughbred butterflies," illustration from In Fairyland—A Series of Pictures from the Elf-World, London, Longmans, Green, Reader & Dyer, 1870
Colored lithograph
7 15/16 x 11 13/16 in.
Gift of Lincoln Kirstein, 1970.565.74

Part of the department's collection of old children's books, this delightful fantasy shows the development of the imagination away from the entertainment of children by means of educational moral tales illustrated with rudimentary woodcuts.

School of Leonardo da Vinci
Late 15th or early 16th c., Italian

Three Heads of Horses
Engraving, first state
4 x 7⅜ in.
Purchase, Bequest of Florance Waterbury, 1970.571

Despite Leonardo's seemingly boundless versatility, he probably did not make any prints himself, but these heads of horses were surely done by someone close to him—the names of Zoan Andrea and Giovanni Antonio da Brescia have been suggested—probably after one of his designs. Only six impressions are known of this state of the engraving, and only five of a second state.

Leonard Bramer
1596–1674, Netherlandish

The Traveling Box
Etching
5⅛ x 7 in.
Harris Brisbane Dick Fund, by exchange, 1970.603.14

This rare print by a follower of Rembrandt is mysterious in its subject matter. Perhaps it is a *vanitas*, as the drawing or print on the wall seems to show a man contemplating the ruins of a once mighty civilization.

Giovanni Domenico Tiepolo
1726–1804, Italian

Picturesque Ideas of the Flight into Egypt
Etching, 1753
7 x 9¼ in.
Purchase, Bequest of Florance Waterbury, 1970.692.1–25

It is said that Tiepolo created his twenty-four scenes of the Holy Family's Flight to prove he could invent an extended sequence of pictures without repeating himself. The set reflects the sparkling achievements of eighteenth-century Venetian etchers as well as young Domenico's flair for the episodic and rustic picturesque.

Pierre Bonnard
1867–1947, French

Illustration in Paul Verlaine's Parallèlement, *published by Ambroise Vollard, Paris, 1900*
Lithograph in rose-colored ink
11⅝ x 9½ in.
The Elisha Whittelsey Collection, the Elisha Whittelsey Fund, 1970.713

Both the format and the use of lithography for book illustration were unusual when Vollard published this edition deluxe, containing 109 exuberant illustrations by Bonnard. It is now considered among the most beautiful illustrated books of all time.

George Bellows
1882–1925, American

In the Park
Lithograph, first state, 1916
Signed by the artist's daughter, Jean Bellows Booth, numbered 22
16 x 21⅛ in.
Fletcher Fund, 1971.514.6

In his lithographs Bellows is most often associated with depictions of boxing, but his peaceful scenes such as this one or his domestic portraits have a quiet power that may prove to be the more lasting.

Josef Albers
Born 1888, American

Family 9 Going Home
Woodcut
Signed in pencil, dated 1933
8¾ x 10 5/16 in.
Gift of the Josef Albers Foundation, Inc.,
1971.636.17

With the gift of over one hundred prints by this artist in 1970 and 1971, the Museum has a complete set of Albers's graphic works, including woodcuts, lithographs, linocuts, and silkscreens, the earliest dating from the 1920s when Albers was teaching at the Bauhaus and had committed himself to the school's program of progressive design and exacting craftsmanship.

Jean Honoré Fragonard
1732–1806, French

Fanfan Playing with Polichinelle and Friends
Etching, 1782
10⅛ x 7⅜ in.
Louis V. Bell and Rogers Funds, and Roland L.
Redmond Gift, 1972.539.1

Fragonard etched this endearing "snapshot" of his two-year-old son, Alexandre, with the help of his young pupil and sister-in-law, Marguerite Gérard. She retained the print in her own print collection, which is the provenance of this and thirty other prints by and after Fragonard that the Museum purchased in 1972.

Arendt van Bolten
Working around 1637, Dutch

Grotesque figures
Plate from a set by an unknown engraver after
Bolten, published by (Pierre?) Firens
5⅞ x 8 in.
Harris Brisbane Dick Fund and The Elisha
Whittelsey Collection, the Elisha Whittelsey
Fund, by exchange 1972.543.3

These monstrosities were imagined by a designer who was also a goldsmith, and whose drawings, dated 1634, are in the British Museum. Although over 300 of these drawings are known, only twenty or so are known to have been engraved. They are seldom found.

Edgar Degas
  1834–1917, French

La Sortie du Bain
  Lithograph, first state, about 1890–1892
  9⅝ x 8¾ in.
  Bequest of Clifford A. Furst and Harris Brisbane Dick Fund, by exchange, 1972.571

Captivated by the spontaneous, natural positions of the female body, Degas spent the better part of his life making pictures of women engaged in the routine activities of daily existence.

Self-portrait
  Etching, first state, 1857–1858
  Signed in pencil
  9 x 5⅝ in.
  Purchase, Mr. and Mrs. Richard J. Bernhard Gift, 1972.625

Guided by Ingres and by Rembrandt, Degas meshed delicate lines with piercing insights into human personality. He was only twenty-three when he etched this portrait, certainly one of the most spellbinding of any age. Only one other impression of this state is known.

Femme nue debout, à sa toilette
  Lithograph, third state, about 1890–1892
  14¾ x 10⅝ in.
  Purchase, Mr. and Mrs. C. Douglas Dillon Gift, 1972.626

In a letter of 1891 Degas spoke of printing a suite of lithographs, a series of female bathers. His project never materialized as such, and we are left with tantalizing glimpses of some of the schemes, like this statuesque nude, described in rich black ink.

Edgar Degas
1834–1917, French

Landscape
> Monotype in oil colors, heightened with pastel
> Signed, lower left, about 1890–1893
> 10 x 13⅜ in.
> Purchase, Mr. and Mrs. Richard J. Bernhard
> Gift, 1972.636

Though the monotype process, by definition, yields but one impression, Degas printed two of this work, adding pastel to achieve varying effects of light, weather, and season. The second impression is in the Museum of Fine Arts, Boston.

La Sortie du Bain
> Crayon électrique, etching, drypoint, and
> aquatint, eleventh to twelfth state, about
> 1882
> 5 x 5 in.
> Harris Brisbane Dick and Rogers Funds and
> The Elisha Whittelsey Collection, the Elisha
> Whittelsey Fund, Bequest of Edwin de T.
> Bechtel, and Gift of Mrs. Bessie Potter
> Vonnoh, by exchange, 1972.659

Degas worked painstakingly through at least seventeen states in the preparation of this plate, perfecting its compact arrangement of shapes and patterns with successive additions of drypoint lines and aquatint.

Giovanni Benedetto Castiglione
About 1610–1663/65, Italian

Diogenes
> Etching, first state, by 1647
> 8½ x 11⅞ in.
> The Elisha Whittelsey Collection, the Elisha
> Whittelsey Fund, 1973.500.1

This so-called "proof before letters" is complete except for a long dedication to the patron Nicolo Simonelli and the address of the publisher. Bartsch calls the print imperfect, saying that Castiglione never finished the arm holding the lantern, but perhaps the artist meant the light from Diogenes' candle to shine back on the philosopher himself. Stoic and Cynical philosophies fascinated Castiglione, and he depicted Diogenes in four media, a painting, a monotype, and this etching, all in the later 1640s, and a brush drawing of about 1660. The ruined columns, priapic herm, and strange animals and vegetation occur again and again in Castiglione's work.

Antonio Canal, called Canaletto
1697–1768, Italian

Capriccio: View of a City
Etching, first state, dated 1741
11¾ x 17⅛ in.
Purchase, Gift of Mary V. T. Eberstadt and
Bequest of Gertrude Moira Flanagan, by ex-
change, 1973.634

Often called an imaginary view of Venice because of the architectural and topographical re-
semblances to La Serenissima, this capriccio also
contains reminiscences of Rome. This state of the
etching is known in only six impressions. The
plate was later divided to make two separate
etchings. It is, except for the title page to his
etchings, the only plate that Canaletto dated.

Jacques Villon
1875–1963, French

Renée de Trois Quart
Drypoint, 1911
Signed in pencil, 16/30
21½ x 16¼ in.
Purchase, Joseph Pulitzer Bequest, 1974.543.3

Our purchase of twenty-seven prints by Villon,
one of the early twentieth century's outstanding
painter-engravers, represents an effort to
strengthen a relatively weak area in the Museum's print collection.

William Merritt Chase
1848–1916, American

Reverie: A Portrait of a Woman
Monotype, about 1890
19 11/32 x 15 13/16 in.
Purchase, Louis V. Bell, Dodge, and Fletcher
Funds, Murray Rafsky Gift, and funds from
various donors, 1974.544

Only recently has interest in the monotype revived, especially as practiced by American artists
of the last quarter of the nineteenth century. Of
unusual size, this sensitive portrait, probably of
Mrs. Chase, catches the artist's flashing brushstrokes at their best.

Edgar Degas
1834–1917, French

La Sortie du Bain
Lithograph, fifth state, about 1890–1892
17 x 19¼ in.
Bequest of Clifford A. Furst, by exchange,
1974.547.1

In this largest of all his lithographs, Degas brings
his oft-repeated bather with falling tresses into
close range and soft focus.

Kurt Schwitters
1887–1948, German

Plate from Merzmappe (Merz Portfolio)
Lithograph, 1923
Signed in pencil, numbered 48, 1
21⅞ x 17½ in.
Bequest of Clifford A. Furst, by exchange,
1974.547.2

"Merz" was a word used freely by Schwitters as
his personal expression of Dada, to denote certain
of his works of art. In 1923 he published *Merzmappe,* six lithographs made in a commercial
printing shop, on paper freshly printed with
images in one color meant to have other colors
superimposed. Schwitters added to these sheets
cutouts of other printed material—silkscreen, cig-
arette wrappers, and the like—all in a geometri-
cized pattern that reflected the style popular with
the artists of the then newly established Bauhaus
in Weimar.

Martin Engelbrecht
1684–1756, German

Sconce with the attributes of Spring
Plate one of a set of sconces representing the
four seasons
Published in Augsburg
Engraving
11⅝ x 7⅞ in.
The Elisha Whittelsey Collection, the Elisha
Whittelsey Fund, 1974.619.3(1)

Published in the eighteenth century in Ausburg
were myriads of prints containing designs for
furniture, metalwork, architectural interiors, and
decorative elements of all varieties.

François Mazot
    Worked around 1650, French

Evening
    Engraving
    11⅝ x 15 in.
    The Elisha Whittelsey Collection, the Elisha
        Whittelsey Fund, 1974.653.1

This picture is, as it says, a fashion plate for
manners and customs as well as for clothing,
furniture, and musical instruments.

Brown & Severin
    American

Barnum's American Museum, New York
    Lithograph, plate and hand colored, 1857
    22¾ x 30 7/16 in.
    Gift of Mary Knight Arnold, 1974.673.105

The group of prints and watercolors given to the
Museum by Mary Knight Arnold supplements the
important collection of New York City views
bequeathed by the late Edward W. C. Arnold.
Barnum's American Museum was famous for its
exhibits as well as its fantastic exterior adver-
tising.

Attributed to **Jan Cornelisz. Vermeyen**
    About 1500–1559, Dutch

A doe and two lionesses
    Etching
    10¼ x 9 1/16 in.
    The Elisha Whittelsey Collection, the Elisha
        Whittelsey Fund, 1975.525

One of Holland's first etchers, Vermeyen produced little but his influence was great, especially
in his use of nonreligious subjects such as this.
It may be that this unrecorded etching, showing
animals not found in Europe, was made during
Vermeyen's sojourn in North Africa in the service
of Emperor Charles V.

Jean-Jacques Le Queu
1757–1825(?), French

Portrait of a Little Girl and Her Dog
Brown watercolor
Signed in ink: J.J.le Queu delin. au S. Republ.
17 x 12⅜ in.
Gift of Mrs. Benjamin Ginsburg, 68.750

This extraordinary portrait of a solemn little face, echoed in the Egyptian-style stone mask, has been done with such loving care that it probably represents the daughter of the artist, who was not a painter but an architect.

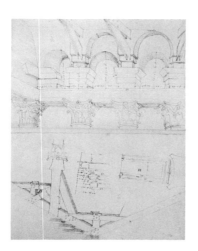

Attributed to Philibert de l'Orme
1505/10–1570, French

Architectural details of the Pantheon, Rome
Pen and brown ink over black chalk on paper
22 x 16¾ in.
Rogers Fund, Joseph Pulitzer Bequest and Mark
J. Millard Gift, 68.769.1

This drawing, on paper whose watermark dates it 1560, shows the antique bronze supports in the porch of the Pantheon that were later replaced with wood when bronze was needed to cast the columns of Bernini's baldachin in Saint Peter's.

Filippo Juvarra
1678–1736, Italian

Architectural fantasy
Pen and brown ink, inscribed "Prospettive Fatti
a 15: Agosto/1704. in Roma"
11⅜ x 8 in.
Rogers Fund, 69.655

This earliest-known dated drawing by the greatest Italian architect of his time is in the only album of his drawings in the United States, one of five outside Italy. Our album contains drawings of his earliest architectural projects in his native city, Messina, as well as some for Lucca; the majority are from his short Roman sojourn (1704–1713) and include two early sketches for his only documented executed architectural work in Rome, the Antamoro Chapel in S. Girolamo della Carità.

Unknown French artist

Design for a ballroom pavilion
   Watercolor and ink
   Inscribed, "Salle de Bal pour un Prince, 1813"
   15⅝ x 30½ in.
   Rogers Fund, 1970.507.1

Formerly attributed to Charles Percier (1764–1838), Napoleon's foremost architect-designer, this drawing, probably by one of his pupils, displays many of the decorative embellishments used by Percier for the festive decorations devised for the marriage of Napoleon and Marie Louise and published in 1810. With its light-hearted and fanciful conglomeration of the neoclassicisms characteristic of the Empire style, and with its pendant, a design for the interior of the pavilion, this is among the most elaborate and eye-pleasing architectural drawings to come to us from the Napoleonic era.

John Sanderson
   Active mid-18th c., British

Design for the decoration of the dining room formerly at Kirtlington Park, Oxfordshire
   Pen, brown and gray ink, and wash over
      graphite
   17⅜ x 20 in.
   Rogers Fund, 1970.674.1

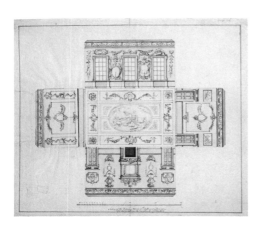

It is not often that a museum, owning a great period room, is able years later to acquire the preparatory drawings for that room. However, this is the case here. The dining room was acquired in 1931, the drawings thirty-nine years later. They must be from an early stage of the planning since none corresponds exactly to the present appearance of the room.

Jean-Jacques Huvé
   1742–1808, French

Elevation for a proposed monument
   Pen, black ink, and wash over graphite, signed
      on verso
   16 x 66 in.
   Gift of Charles B. Wrightsman, 1970.736.51

The pyramidal mausoleum is flanked by extensive Doric colonnades terminating in stepped-domed pavilions; on the pyramid is a bas-relief of a head in profile crowned with laurel. This allusion to a literary figure suggests that this is possibly a monument to Voltaire, to whom a number of monuments in comparable style were dedicated during this period.

Austrian School (?)
  18th c.

Designs for embroidery of an orphrey and a chasuble
  Pen and brush in brown ink on paper
  54½ x 11¼ and 61½ x 18⅞ in.
  Harris Brisbane Dick Fund and Joseph Pulitzer Bequest, 1971.513.93a,b

These full-scale designs for the embroidery of ecclesiastical vestments must have formed part of a library of such patterns. The orphrey illustrates fables concerning animals and birds.

Thomas Chippendale
  1718–1779, English

Ribband back Chairs, No. 16
  Pen and ink, gray wash, about 1754
  7⅜ and 13⅜ in.
  Rogers Fund, 1972.581

One of the more famous English cabinetmakers, Chippendale is also noted for his *Gentleman and Cabinet-Maker's Director,* first published in 1754. This drawing is for Plate XVI of that edition. A set of four side chairs, the gift of Edwin C. Vogel to the Museum in 1957, closely relates to the center chair in the drawing.

Frank Lloyd Wright
  1868–1959, American

West elevation of the Francis W. Little House
  Pencil on tissue, about 1912
  23¼ x 42½ in.
  Purchase, Emily C. Chadbourne Bequest, 1972.607.1

The group of drawings accompanying the Museum's acquisition of a room and architectural elements from this house are significant additions to its growing collection of American architectural drawings.   DWK

Workshop of Giuseppe Bibiena
1695–1757, Italian

Design for a catafalque for Le Grand Dauphin
Pen and brown ink with brown and gray wash
on the statues
29¼ x 20 7/16 in.
Bequest of Joseph H. Durkee, by exchange,
1972.713.46

This sumptuous and elegant design comes from
a group of seventy-two drawings associated with
members of the Bibiena family, Italy's greatest
family of designers for theater and festival. The
majority of the group is associated with Ferdi-
nando Bibiena, Principal Theater Architect at the
Imperial Austrian court, and his son, Giuseppe,
who succeeded him in the post.

Jean Charles Delafosse
1734–1791, French

Elevation and end wall of a "Grande Galerie"
Pen, gray ink, and wash with traces of brown
wash over black chalk
Signed and dated, lower left, "J.C. Delafosse
Inv. faite 1769"
14¾ x 32½ in.
Purchase Joseph Pulitzer Bequest, 1973.638

Delafosse, an architect and designer of ornament,
was an important neoclassic stylist; his influence
derived especially from his enormous publication, the *Nouvelle Iconologie Historique* (1768).
This drawing includes many of the distinctive
elements of his style seen in his book—trophies,
vases, friezes, and swags—combined in a monumental ensemble. The large size of the drawing,
rare in Delafosse's oeuvre, affords a dazzling
view of a Louis XVI Grande Galerie.

Twentieth Century Art

Comments by Henry Geldzahler, Curator (HG), Penelope Hunter, Curatorial Assistant, Western European Arts (PH), and Jean Mailey, Associate Curator, Textile Study Room (JM)

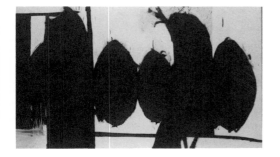

Robert Motherwell
1915– , American

Elegy to the Spanish Republic, 70, 1961
Oil on canvas
69 x 114 in.
Anonymous Gift, 65.247

The artist dislikes *La Danse II*, which we acquired by purchase in 1953. Since then we have been given four of his best paintings, of which this is one. HG

Max Weber
1881–1961, American

Athletic Contest
Oil on canvas
40 x 55¼ in.
George A. Hearn Fund, 67.112

A cubist rebus of great complexity but ultimately a legible and energetic composition, this is one of Weber's most ambitious works. HG

Jules Pascin
  1885–1930, American

Semi-Nude
  Oil on canvas
  39½ x 32 in.
  Bequest of Miss Adelaide Milton de Groot
    (1876–1967), 67.187.168

This fine painting by the Bulgarian-born, Paris-trained artist shows him in the tender, lyrical, somewhat dejected mood he captured so well at such great personal cost.   HG

Morris Louis
  1912–1962, American

Alpha Pi, 1960
  Acrylic on canvas
  102½ x 177 in.
  Arthur Hoppock Hearn Fund, 67.232

When we purchased this heroic painting, I consulted with the critic and art historian Michael Fried on its selection. It is considered one of our major postwar American paintings and a key example of the artist's style.   HG

Pierre Bonnard
  1867–1947, French

The Terrace at Vernon
  Oil on canvas
  57 11/16 x 76½ in.
  Gift of Mrs. Frank Jay Gould, 68.1

One of our most important European paintings of the twentieth century, this is extraordinarily beautiful in its perfectly modulated range of colors that are typical of Bonnard in his post-Nabi years. The composition is one of the artist's most complex, including a vignette of the two figures in conversation at the extreme left and the Maillol-like attitude of the woman on the right. All this action is perfectly melded with the brilliant landscape. Painted between 1930 and 1938, the work is both postimpressionist and neoclassic.
                    HG

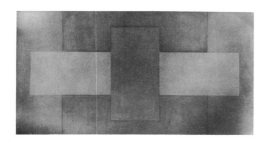

Ad Reinhardt
1913–1967, American

Red Painting
Oil on canvas
78 x 144 in.
Arthur Hoppock Hearn Fund, 68.85

This, the largest of the artist's red paintings, was purchased within a year of his death. Reinhardt is well known for his late black paintings, which I hope one day will be represented in the collection. The present work, much admired by younger artists, is one that is often requested for loan to exhibitions at other institutions.   HG

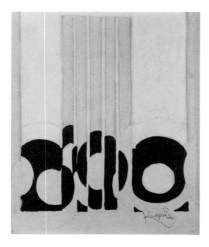

Frank Kupka
1871–1957, Czechoslovakian

Disques Noirs Syncopés
Gouache and pencil on paper
9 13/16 x 7⅞ in.
Rogers Fund, 68.108

I saw this small, exquisite gouache at Spencer Samuel's Gallery in 1968 and used our discretionary funds for the year to purchase it. It has been on view only once because the galleries available to the Twentieth Century Art Department are on such a grand scale that they make the showing of small works a problem. We hope someday soon to have the space and architectural flexibility to exhibit large paintings, small works, and furniture in a suite of galleries that can accommodate such versatile installations.   HG

Morton Schamberg

1881–1918, American

Four untitled drawings
Pencil on paper
5½ x 4½, 5 5/16 x 4½, 7 3/16 x 4⅝, 7¼ x 4 11/16
in.
Purchase, The Bertram F. and Susie Brummer
Foundation, Inc. Gift, 68.115.1-4

These inventive, fully realized miniature drawings are the first works by Schamberg to enter
the collection. His death in the influenza epidemic
of 1918 was a tragic loss to American art.   HG

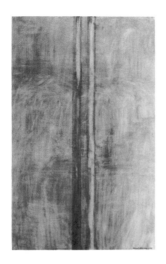

Barnett Newman
1905–1970, American

Concord
 Oil and masking tape on canvas
 89¾ x 53⅝ in.
 George A. Hearn Fund, 68.178

Concord, painted in 1949 and first exhibited in 1950, is an example of Newman's work at its best. For years he had a reputation as an artist's artist, and it was not until the late fifties and early sixties that he was seen more generally as a major contributor to the glory of postwar American art. Although *Concord* is the only representation of Newman's work in the Museum, it stands as a major statement in the history of American abstraction.   HG

John Graham
1881?–1961, American

Celia
 Oil, casein, charcoal, chalk, pencil, pen, ink on
  composition board
 48 x 36 in.
 Hugo Kastor Fund, 68.185

Graham (born Dabrowsky) was a Russian who came to America in the 1920s. He befriended Arshile Gorky and Willem de Kooning in their formative years, and there was unquestionably a cross-influence in their work in the thirties. *Celia,* one of Graham's handsomest portraits, is, a few short decades after its execution, a difficult painting to date with absolute conviction. Let us say it was probably painted in the forties and that it has an eccentric dignity reminiscent of Roman portraiture and Ingres, plus a hint of biomorphic surrealism.   HG

Ellsworth Kelly
1923–   , American

Spectrum V
 Oil on canvas
 Each panel 84¼ x 34¼ in.
 Gift of Ellsworth Kelly, 69.210.1–13

The artist's largest painting, this was first seen during our exhibition *New York Painting and Sculpture 1940–1970.* Both Kelly and I felt that one of his *Spectrums,* a recent and impressive development in his work, should be included. The City Art Museum of St. Louis declined to lend theirs, whereupon the artist painted this one. It requires forty to sixty feet of wall space, depending on the distance between the panels, a distance that has not been permanently fixed by the artist or by experience.   HG

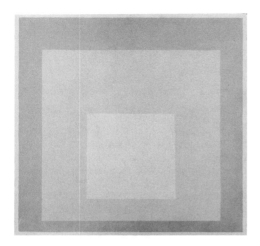

Josef Albers
  1888– , American

Homage to the Square: Green Promise
  Oil on masonite
  24 x 24 in.
Homage to the Square: Enfolding
  Oil on canvas
  24 x 24 in.
  Gift of Josef Albers, 69.274.1–2

The artist's work is more varied than his best-known series, *Homage to the Square,* might suggest. Even within the apparently self-limiting format the variation in mood and expressiveness is great, and those examples that have entered our collection indicate this forcefully. The titles are not arbitrary: they are carefully chosen and apt.

                             HG

Morris Louis
  1912–1962, American

Beth Chet (1958)
  Acrylic on canvas
  91⅛ x 137½ in.
  Gift of Mrs. Abner Brenner, 69.276

The gift of this painting by the artist's widow was in part an acknowledgment of our recognition of the artist's importance, which we had made clear with the purchase of *Alpha Pi* two years previously. *Beth Chet,* a bronze veil, shows Louis to advantage at another, earlier stylistic moment in his career as a color-field painter. We anticipate the gift of a Louis *Pillar,* painted in the last years of his life, which will give us a representative selection of a great American artist at his best.

                             HG

Robert Motherwell
 1915– , American

Open No. 19 in blue
  Oil on canvas
  84 x 115½ in.
Open No. 35, raw umber on sized canvas
  Polymer paint and charcoal on canvas
  76 x 114 in.
Open No. 37 in orange with charcoal line
  Polymer paint and charcoal on canvas
  88 x 122 in.
  Anonymous Gift, 69.277.1–3

These works share the rectangular motif common to the series but each evokes in a different way the architecture, landscape, and sky from which its imagery is distilled.   HG

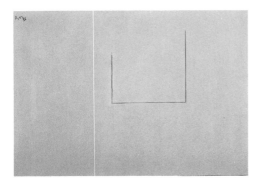

Georgia O'Keeffe
    1887–   , American

Black Iris
    Oil on canvas
    36 x 29⅞ in.
Black Abstraction
    Oil on canvas
    30 x 40¼ in.
Blue Lines No. 10
    Watercolor
    24 15/16 x 18 15/16
Abstraction IX
    Charcoal
    24¼ x 18¾ in.
    The Alfred Stieglitz Collection, Gift of Georgia
        O'Keeffe, 69.278.1–4

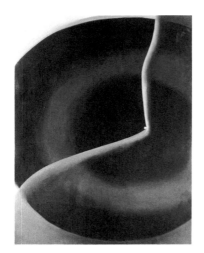

These works had been on deposit at the Museum since 1949, the year in which Miss O'Keeffe arranged for the gift to the Museum of a large portion of the Alfred Stieglitz Bequest. *Black Iris*, painted in 1926, is a particularly fine example of her work, and the two drawings, dated 1916, are among the earliest indications of her original style. With the gift of these works we now have fifteen O'Keeffe paintings, drawings, and watercolors.   HG

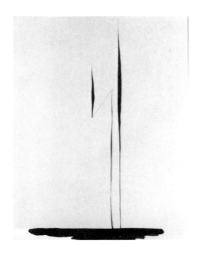

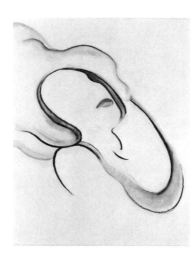

Edward Avedisian
1936–   , American

Kool Aid
Acrylic on canvas
75½ x 112¾ in.
George A. Hearn Fund, 1970.79

One of two Avedisians in the collection. Avedisian has been exhibiting abstract painting in New York since 1959, soon after he moved here from Boston. The striking paint quality, original color sense, and sheer intensity make this one of the outstanding works by an artist of his generation to enter the collection. Avedisian's community of interest with postwar European abstraction stands as a challenge to the narrowness of much recent American taste   HG

Wassily Kandinsky
1866–1944, Russian

Free Curve to the Point
Pen and India ink
15¾ x 11⅞ in.
Rogers Fund, 1970.99

An illustration for the artist's pedagogic book *Point and Line* (1925), this exquisite work will be on view more often when we have the flexibility to show works that are small and sensitive to natural light.   HG

Josef Albers
1888–   , American

Pillars
Sandblasted flashed glass
11¾ x 12¼ in.
George A. Hearn Fund, 1970.139

Made in the late 1920s, *Pillars* is in the linear style by which we know this artist.   HG

Mark Rothko

1903–1970, American

Reds No. 16, 1960
  Oil on canvas
  102 x 119½ in.
  Arthur Hoppock Hearn Fund, George A. Hearn
    Fund, and Hugo Kastor Fund, 1971.14

This work traveled from New York to a collector
in Brussels and back to New York, where I saw
it in the mid-sixties. I long wanted it for the
collection, and it was prominently displayed in
New York Painting and Sculpture 1940–1970.
More than any other painting in the collection of
the Twentieth Century Art Department, *Reds*
depends on the right lighting conditions to bring
out the richly glowing harmonies of its deep, dark
colors.   HG

Hans Hofmann

1880–1966, American
The Renate Series

Rhapsody
  Oil on canvas
  84¼ x 60½ in.
  Gift of Renate Hofmann, 1975
Lonely Journey
  Oil on canvas
  50 x 49¼ in.
Little Cherry
  Oil on canvas
  85¼ x 78⅜ in.
Legends of Distant Past Days
  Oil on canvas
  40¼ x 50¼ in.
Heraldic Call
  Oil on canvas
  61⅛ x 60⅛ in.
Profound Longing
  Oil on canvas
  50⅛ x 40 1/16 in.
Deep Within the Ravine
  Oil on canvas
  84⅛ x 60⅜ in.
Summer, 1965
  Oil on canvas
  H. 72 x 48 in.
Lust and Delight
  Oil on canvas
  84¼ x 60¼ in.
  Loan, Promised Gift of Renate Hofmann,
    L.1971.49.2–9

In 1965, when he was eighty-five and at the height
of his power as an artist, Hans Hofmann painted

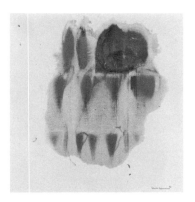

this series and dedicated it to his young wife, Renate. Much of his power, joy, and stylistic scope can be inferred from these nine paintings in which his life's experience with cubist drawing and structure, and his hard-won freedom and originality in color are triumphantly evident. The miracle in these paintings is as much in the artist's sure sense of when to desist as it is in their fullness and richness. Hofmann knew when to leave a painting at the moment of greatest freedom. We are grateful to Renate Hofmann for her generosity and proud that all of these important works will enter the Museum's collection. HG

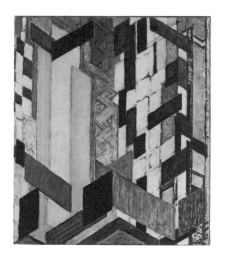

Frank Kupka
1871–1957, Czechoslovakian

Plans Par Verticales
Oil on canvas
24⅛ x 19¾ in.
Gift of Joseph H. Hazen Foundation, Inc.,
1971.111

The collection is notoriously weak in the European art of this century. We can, of course, make no attempt to duplicate or compete with the Museum of Modern Art's staggering collection of European modern art. We should, however, as a persuasive encyclopaedic museum, have key works by the best artists to make the crucial point that the history of art is continuous. Postwar American painting is inexplicable without its European predecessors. And it cannot be adequately judged without comparison to its European contemporaries. Kupka's *Plans Par Verticales* was therefore a welcome gift.   HG

Josef Albers
1888–   , American

Rheinische Legende
Glass shards on copper sheet
19½ x 17½ in.
Figure
Glass shards on brass sheet
21½ x 15½ in.
Gift of Josef Albers, 1972.40.1–2

These works of 1921, from the glassworking shop at the Bauhaus, are early yet mature creations.

Indicating Solids
Oil on masonite
26 x 25¾ in.

Variant: 6 Greens
  Oil on masonite
  39⅞ x 37 in.
Variant: 2 Whites, 2 Yellows, 2 Greens
  Oil on masonite
  39⅞ x 37 in.
  Gift of Josef Albers, 1972.40.3–5

Indicating Solids, 1949, is a completely successful essay in grayed variations. The Variants, begun in 1947 and 1948, are strong abstractions with architectural and landscape references.

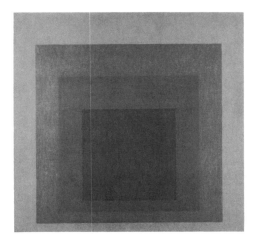

Homage to the Square: Dilated
  Oil on masonite
  48 x 48 in.
Homage to the Square: Soft Spoken
  Oil on masonite
  48 x 48 in.
Homage to the Square: On Near Sky
  Oil on masonite
  48 x 48 in.

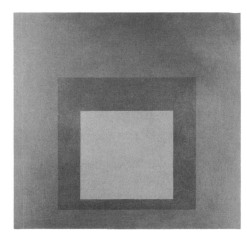

Josef Albers
   1888–   , American

Never Before
   Oil on masonite
   48 x 48 in.
   Gift of Josef Albers, 1972.40.6–9

Like *Indicating Solids*, this work of 1971 is an essay in grayed variations, an irregular four-sided figure on a divided background.

Homage to the Square: Frontal Backing
   Oil on Masonite
   40 x 40 in.
Transformation of a Scheme No. 8
   Engraving on formica
   17 x 22 7/16 in.
Transformation of a Scheme No. 9
   Engraving on formica
   17 x 22⅞ in.
   Gift of Josef Albers, 1972.40.10–12

These works of 1949 and 1950 show the artist manipulating perspective in a poetry that goes beyond mere design while preserving the two-dimensionality that has continued to fascinate him.   HG

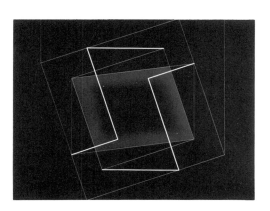

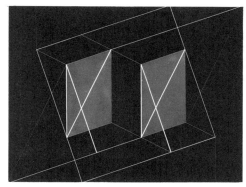

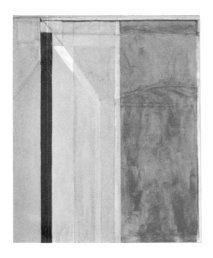

Richard Diebenkorn
1922–   , American

Ocean Park #30
Oil on canvas
100 x 82 in.
Bequest of Miss Adelaide Milton de Groot
(1876–1967), by exchange, 1972.126

Diebenkorn is a fine painter in California (first in San Francisco for many years, now in Los Angeles) whose reputation is well deserved and growing. From the mid-fifties to the mid-sixties he produced memorable figurative paintings, which, like his more recent abstractions, owe something to the compositional and color sense of Matisse.   HG

David Hockney
1937–   , English

Mt. Fuji and Flowers
Acrylic on canvas
60 x 48 in.
Purchase, Mrs. Arthur Hays Sulzberger Gift,
1972.128

Hockey's work combines wit, keen observation, and artistic imagination. I had known the artist for years and waited to purchase a work for the Museum until I saw the right painting. I was in his studio in London in 1972 and *Mt. Fuji and Flowers* had just been finished. I slapped a reserve on it and we acquired it within months of its execution from the Andrê Emmerich Gallery, where it was shown for the first time. Lent to Hockney's retrospective at the Musée des Arts Decoratifs in 1974, it was one of the most admired canvases in the exhibition.   HG

Hans Hartung
1904–   , German

T 1965–E–33
Acrylic on canvas
60⅝ x 98½ in.
Purchase, Bequest of Miss Adelaide Milton de
Groot (1876–1967), by exchange, 1972.129

There has been a tendency in postwar America to deride, or at least to underestimate, the accomplishments of the contemporary School of Paris. Hartung's work of the past decade is virtually unknown in America; this painting of 1965, painted at the same time as Jules Olitski's spray paintings, arrives independently at similar expressions.   HG

Phillip Guston
1913– , American

Close-Up III
Oil on canvas
70 x 72 in.
Gift of Lee V. Eastman, 1972.281

We acquired an early figurative Guston, *The Performers,* in 1950. *Close-Up III,* a gift I shamelessly solicited, is the first abstract painting by him in the collection. We have since purchased a handsome ink drawing of 1960 from the artist. An abstract of the mid-fifties and one of his recent paintings—figurative in an unexpected way that has yet to meet with general critical understanding—would give us an impressive sampling of Guston's work.   HG

Larry Poons
1937– , American

No. 23
Acrylic on canvas
95 x 125 in.
George A. Hearn Fund, 1973.66

This painting was acquired within a year of its execution, with the advice of Clement Greenberg. It is a fine example of the artist's recent manner. It consists of thickly applied acrylic paint, brownish in overall tonality, which makes the relatively bright blue and yellow of the upper left-hand corner delicious and exciting. Someday we hope to acquire, through purchase or gift, an earlier Poons in which small circles or ellipses of color hover on a single background color in patterns that establish a fine balance between randomness and logic.   HG

Paul Klee
1879–1940, Swiss

Le Kash-Né
Oil on paper
13 x 8½ in.
Gift of Mr. and Mrs. William L. McKim, 1973.213

The title, phonetically, amounts to the French for nose-guard. A witty, colorful, though minor, example of Klee's work, it is the first painting by the artist to enter the collection. It came as a complete surprise; a gentleman telephoned for an appointment and came to the office with the small oil under his arm. He had bought it in the late thirties from the dealer Kurt Valentin for several hundred dollars. Did we want it? We did.
                    HG

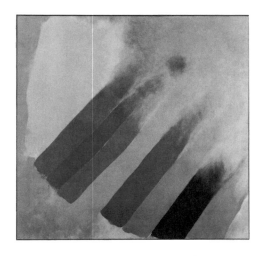

Friedel Dzubas
1915– , American

Fan Tan
Magna on canvas
96 x 96 in.
George A. Hearn Fund, 1973.316

As with the Poons and the Avedesian, Dzubas's *Fan Tan* was acquired within a year of its execution. There is a reason to this pattern: all the artists have been well known to me for at least twelve years, and in each case I felt that a recent painting was among the best they had yet done. The decorative zest of *Fan Tan* and its perfect amalgam of flat and misty paint application make it an eminently likable painting of immediate and lasting impact. HG

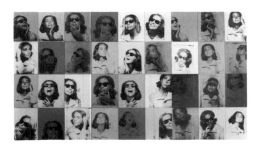

Andy Warhol
1930– , American

Ethel Scull 36 Times
Silkscreen on canvas
100 x 144 in.
Loan, Promised Gift of Mr. and Mrs. Robert C. Scull, L.1974.10

As pop art is virtually unrepresented at the Museum, we are delighted with this promised gift of the artist's earliest and best portrait. HG

Isamu Noguchi
1904– , American

Study for Worksheet (1945)
Collage: graph paper with cutouts of black construction paper, penciled outlines
Collage proper: 17 x 22 in.
Purchase, Rogers Fund and Sumner Foundation Gift, 1974.200

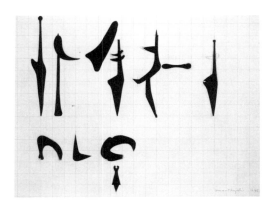

These are sculptor's drawings, a worksheet that reveals both the choreographic and anthropomorphic aspects of Noguchi's inspiration. Sculptural ideas dance across the page, and each is laid down with an elegant regard for its neighbors and for the whole sheet. Noguchi's sculptural vocabulary is exquisitely revealed. HG

Ilya Bolotowsky
1907– , American

Study for W.P.A. Mural
Gouache on academy board
10 x 22 in.
Arthur Hoppock Hearn Fund, 1974.323

An elegant study, this early work sensitively combines the biomorphic forms of the period with intimations of the neo-Mondrian artist Bolotowsky was to become. We became aware of this work through his 1974 retrospective exhibition at the Guggenheim Museum and purchased it at the time.   HG

Ludwig Sander
1906– , American

Cherokee III
Oil on canvas
60 x 65 in.
Gift of Mr. and Mrs. Eugene M. Schwartz, 1974.376.2

Two of this artist's paintings entered our collection within several months of each other, *Cherokee III* by gift, *Rappahanock IV* by purchase. They are very different in format and in color—*Cherokee III* a square in reds and blues, *Rappahanock IV* a horizontal painting in a range of yellows. Of the painters who have worked in the neoplastic tradition, Sander has been the most original. He has arrived at unique solutions to problems of color and juxtaposition that still plague many younger "hard-edge" painters.   HG

John Storrs
1885–1956, American

Forms in Space No. 1
Metals in combination
H. (without base) 20¼ in.
Francis Lathrop Fund, 67.238

We purchased this sculpture, inspired by the stylized American Beaux-Arts skyscrapers of the twenties, almost immediately after I first saw Storrs's work at Edith Halpert's Downtown Gallery in 1967. Storrs was a Chicagoan who worked for decades in France. He exhibited occasionally in his lifetime, but it is only in recent years that his work has become relatively well known.   HG

John Storrs
1885–1956, American

Tête-à-Tête
  Bronze
  11 x 11½ in.
  Edward C. Moore Fund and Rogers Fund,
    1970.10

Acquired after *Forms in Space No. 1*, this work, in its fully modeled round forms, shows another aspect of the artist's style.   HG

David Smith
1906–1965, American

Becca
  Stainless steel
  113¼ x 123 in.
  Bequest of Miss Adelaide Milton de Groot
    (1876–1967), by exchange, 1972.127

Becca (named after the artist's daughter Rebecca) was first exhibited at the Museum's show *New York Painting and Sculpture 1940–1970*, where it stood at the head of the grand staircase at the entrance to the galleries. Smith is internationally recognized as the sculptor whose achievement equals and parallels the great postwar American developments in painting. In this late work, a superb three-dimensional mate to Jackson Pollock's *Autumn Rhythm* and Morris Louis's *Alpha Pi,* one can read Smith's debt to cubism.   HG

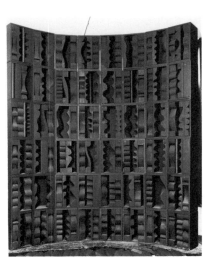

Louise Nevelson
1900– , American

Black Crescent
  Painted wood
  133½ x 86 in.
  Gift of Albert and Vera List, 1972.220

Black Crescent has been shown in six museums since it came to us, only a year after its execution. It is typical of Nevelson's best recent work, a carefully articulated and additive accumulation that derives in scale and imagery from architectural elements. It is the first sculpture by the artist to enter the collection.   HG

Wilhelm Lehmbruck
1881–1919, German

Small Female Torso
Bronze
H. 27½ in.
Gift of Mrs. Maurice E. Blin, 1973.313

Like Paul Klee's *Le Kash-Né,* this lovely sculpture came as a surprise gift, and, like the Klee, it was originally purchased from the dealer Kurt Valentin. It was a welcome gift indeed, as we are weak in non-French sculpture of the first decades of this century. Though it owes something to Rodin, Despiau, and Maillol as well as to the cult of the antique, it has an introspective grace characteristic of this artist at his best.   HG

Raoul Hague
1904– , American

Big Indian Mountain
Walnut
H. 64 in.
Louis V. Bell Fund, 1974.6

Had I known the fully realized nature of Hague's mature work at the time of *New York Painting and Sculpture 1940–1970,* I would surely have included him in the exhibition. In 1972 I saw a monumental carved wooden piece at Virginia Zabriskie's gallery and arranged with her to visit the artist's studio in Woodstock. Help on this acquisition came from several colleagues: the Chairman of Greek and Roman Art thought it looked like a Lion of Delos, and the Chairman of Western European Arts saw in it the amplitude and energy of Baroque sculpture. I thank them for their convincing support.   HG

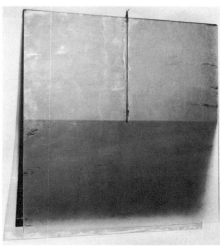

Christopher Wilmarth
1943– , American

Beginning
Etched glass, steel plate, wire rope
40 x 40 in.
Rogers Fund, 1974.18

Wilmarth's work is powerful and evocative; its structural elements are distinct; this apparent simplicity conceals much adjustment and simplification; the way in which the etched glass diffuses the light accounts, in part, for its memorable poetic effect.   HG

Carlo Bugatti
1855–1940, Italian

Secretary with mirror
About 1888–1902
Walnut, pewter, copper, vellum
88 x 39½ in.
Purchase, Edward C. Moore, Jr., Gift, 69.69

Father of the automobile designer and an animal sculptor, Bugatti was in his own right the most extraordinary furniture designer in Italy at the turn of the century. PH

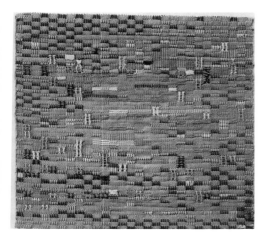

Anni Albers
1899– , American

Pasture
1958
Cotton compound tabby panel patterned with various combinations of double weave, warp and weft floats, gauze and soumak detail
15½ x 14 in.
Purchase, Edward C. Moore Fund, 69.135

Mrs. Albers, who came to this country with her husband in the late 1930s, is one of the most prominent weavers of the twentieth century. *Pasture* is a relatively late work in a career that began when the artist was a student at the Bauhaus. The weaving is both richly textured and clearly articulated. HG

James Prestini
1908– , American

Bowl (one of a collection of sixteen)
Curly maple
D. 10 11/16 in.
Gift of James Prestini, 69.164.11

James Prestini, a research engineer by profession, explored the potential of the grain and color of wood turned on a lathe in useful forms of poignant simplicity. His work has with equal success evolved into abstract sculpture. PH

Carlo Bugatti
1855–1940, Italian

Settee
  About 1888–1902
  Walnut, brass, pewter, vellum, silk
  58 x 101 in.
  Rogers Fund, 1970.181.1

Bugatti's works are flights of fantasy incorporating brush painting, metalwork, inlay, and tasseled fringe in a medley of exoticisms.　　PH

Maurice Marinot
1882–1960, French

Covered vase
  About 1925
  Glass
  H. 12 in.
Jar
  1927
  Glass
  H. 9 in.
Bottle
  About 1925–1929
  Glass
  H. 4¾ in.
  Rogers Fund, 1970.198.1a,b,2,3,

A fauve painter, Marinot became enamored of glass as an animate material on a visit to a glasshouse owned by a friend. He soon passed beyond craftsmanship, pushing his glass by experiment and improvisation to new creative dimensions. The eye penetrates the clear, heavy walls of his jar to glimpse a fleshy core behind a fissured tissue of salts. In his covered vase he has fixed the moment of the glassblower's triumph, forming in a monumental shape the still-living material, the trapped air bubbles swirling in resistance.　　PH

Jacques-Emile Ruhlmann
1879–1933, French

Cabinet
   About 1920–1930
   Amboyna and ivory
   52½ x 35½ in.
   Rogers Fund, 1970.198.4

Ruhlmann was acknowledged by colleagues, press, and public as the leading figure in the French decorative movement of the 1920s, now known as art déco. His work provided a distillation of the techniques and forms of French cabinetmaking.   PH

Bedside table
   About 1920–1930
   Macassar ebony and ivory
   26 x 19 in.
   Rogers Fund, 1970.198.5

Ruhlmann used exotic materials such as Macassar ebony and ivory from what were still French colonies to achieve subtly sumptuous decorative effects.   PH

Jean Puiforcat
   1898–1945, French

Covered bowl
   About 1930–1940
   Silver and silver-gilt
   D. 10⅞ in.
   Purchase, Edgar Kaufmann Gift, 1972.5

Were his father not a silversmith, Jean Puiforcat might have been a mathematician or a sculptor. As it was, he was both, by way of being the greatest silversmith of our century.   PH

Josef Hoffmann
1870–1956, Austrian

Three bowls and tray
About 1920
Brass
D. (tray) 12½ in.
Rogers Fund, 1972.177.1–4

Hoffmann was a founder of the Wiener Werk-staette, a craft league active 1903–1932. Following the league ethic that the value of a work lay in the design and craftsmanship rather than the costliness of the material, he wrought similar showpieces in the base metal brass and the precious metal silver.   PH

Pierre Legrain
1888–1929, French

Stool
About 1922–1929
Rosewood
13 x 29 in.
Fletcher Fund, 1972.283.1

African art made a profound impact of the avant garde of Europe in the 1910s and 20s. Legrain interpreted the African influence in furniture commissioned by Jacques Doucet for the apartment that was to house his collection of contemporary art.   PH

Clement Rousseau
1872–   , French

Table
1924
Ebony, ivory, sharkskin
29½ x 18½ in.
Fletcher Fund, 1972.283.2

Rousseau's creation is an ideogram of a portable table whose legs form handles. Its delicacy belies the sturdy structure and the impermeability of its sharkskin surfaces.   PH

Jacques-Emile Ruhlmann
1879–1933, French

Desk, chair, and file cabinet
1918–1919
Amboyna, ivory, sharkskin, leather, silvered
bronze
Desk: 37¼ x 47½ in.
Chair: 29⅝ x 19¼ in.
Cabinet: 27½ x 16½ in.
Purchase, Edgar Kaufmann Gift, 1973.154.1
Bequest of Mr. and Mrs. Graham F. Blandy,
Bequest of Jeanne King de Rham in memory
of her father, David King, and Gift of Vera
Bloom in memory of her father, Congressman
Sol Bloom, by exchange, 1973.154.2
Bequest of Collis P. Huntington, by exchange,
1973.154.3

David David-Weill, a financier, art collector, and
patron of French museums, furnished his home
with French eighteenth-century art. He commissioned Ruhlmann to design a functional desk and
cabinet within this esthetic. They are shown with
a contemporary chair by Ruhlmann whose front
legs and back rail are formed in a continuous
double curve.   PH

Antonio Gaudí
1852–1926, Spanish

Armchair
About 1902–1904
Walnut
38 x 25½ x 20½ in.
Purchase, Joseph H. Hazen Foundation, Inc.
Gift, 1974.107

The vision of the architect Gaudí encompassed
every detail of his buildings, including their furniture. This chair, designed for the Calvet apartment house, is imbued with the almost surreal
organic quality peculiar to Guadí's work.   PH

Chunghi Choo
1938–   , Korean

Panel
Brown silk organza with stitch-resist and tie-
dye pattern in shades of ochre and vermillion
93 x 30¼ in.
Gift of Miss Chunghi Choo, 1974.279

A technique that reached outstanding heights in
the robe decorations of Momoyama Japan is here
directed toward a very different end by a Korean
artist-craftswoman in the 1960s in America.   JM

Jean Dunand
1877–1942, French

Panel depicting a seated black woman
About 1928–1930, signed
Lacquer on wood with patinated copper
37 x 25 in.
Gift of Peter M. Brant, 1974.373.4

Dunand's adaptation of the time-consuming oriental technique of pictorial lacquerwork achieved
such popular success that he was obliged to hire
up to a hundred Indochinese assistants to execute
commissions that ranged to several stories in
height. The subject of this panel provides yet
another example of the place held by blacks, both
African and American, in the popular imagination of Paris in the 1920s.   PH

Vase
About 1920–1930, signed
Copper and plated gold
H. 18 in.
Collection of Stanley Siegel, Gift of Stanley
    Siegel, 1975.72.2

Dunand's early ambition lay in sculpture, but it
was as a coppersmith and later a lacquerer that
he was to earn renown. This majestic vase was
beaten up out of a thin sheet of copper, resist-
electroplated with geometric motifs in gold, then
patinated to a rich variegated amber.   PH

James Prestini
1908– , American

Salad set
1939
Mahogany
D. (tray) 22 in.
Gift of James Prestini, 1975.135.1–8

"During February 1969 when you [Henry Geld-
zahler] were in Berkeley to select examples of my
work for the Metropolitan's collection I did not
show what I consider to be one of my very best
designs as I was not ready to part with it at the
time." Six years later Prestini gave us this set,
designed and made with such precision that the
bowls, touching each other, just fit within the
raised lip of the tray.   PH

Western European Arts

Comments by   Olga Raggio, Chairman of the Department (OR), Yvonne Hackenbroch and James Parker, Curators (YH, JP), Jessie McNab, James David Draper, Clare Le Corbeiller, and Clare Vincent, Associate Curators (JMcN, JDD, CLC, CV), Johanna Hecht and Penelope Hunter, Curatorial Assistants (JH, PH), Jean Mailey, Associate Curator, Textile Study Room (JM), and Edith Appleton Standen, Consultant, Textile Study Room (EAS)

Andrea Briosco, called Riccio
About 1470/75–1532, Italian (Padua)

Seated Satyr
About 1520
Bronze, eyes silvered
H. 9¼ in.
Gift of Irwin Untermyer, 64.101.1417

An intensely personal evocation of classical antiquity, the satyr gazes wistfully while holding a shell-shaped lamp in one hand, his pipes in the other. It is an autograph Riccio of which several variants are known, and among his monuments is perhaps nearest in style to certain figures in the della Torre reliefs (Louvre), about 1516–1521.

JDD

Horse and Rider Startled by a Snake
Early 16th c., north Italian
Bronze
H. 10 in.
Gift of Irwin Untermyer, 64.101.1419

The subject is no doubt a Roman warrior and the scene an actual event of ancient history not yet discovered. The crisp and refined details point to a North Italian goldsmith rather than to Riccio, to whom the group has been traditionally attributed. It is inspired, however, by Riccio's celebrated *Horse and Rider* in the Victoria and Albert Museum.

JDD

231

Dido
　Mid-17th c., probably Flemish
　Bronze, on "Boulle" base of wood inlaid with
　　pewter and tortoiseshell
　H. 9 in.
　Gift of Irwin Untermyer, 64.101.1466

The figure's crown identifies the subject as Queen Dido of Carthage, stabbing herself with the (missing) sword of Aeneas after her abandonment by him. While the voluptuous physical type is clearly Rubensian, the sweeping movement and high pitch of drama indicate close acquaintance with the art of Bernini and the Roman baroque. Other casts are in the Victoria and Albert Museum and the Bayerisches Nationalmuseum, Munich.　　　　　　　　　　　　　　　JDD

Neptune
　Second half of 16th c., south German
　Bronze
　H. 15 in.
　Gift of Irwin Untermyer, 64.101.1547

With its spouted base (thus clearly from a table fountain), this has all the vigor and humor that characterize the best of sixteenth-century German bronze statuettes.　　　　　　　　　　JDD

Attributed to Salvatore Franco and others
　18th c., Italian (Naples)

Nativity with Angels
　Second half of 18th c.
　Polychromed terracotta and wood with tow-
　　wrapped wire torsos, silk clothes, silver-gilt
　　ornaments
　Gift of Loretta Hines Howard, 64.164.1–167

Shown is part of the great *presepio* and glory of angels displayed each year at the Museum's Christmas tree. The exquisitely rendered beatific expressions and gracefully angled heads of these *crèche* figures, with their masses of hair swept up as if by the breath of some unseen spirit, support the presumption that they are the work of some of Naples's most gifted sculptors.
　　　　　　　　　　　　　　　　　　　JH

Robert Le Lorrain
1666–1743, French

Bacchante and Young Satyr
Early 18th c.
Lead
H. 78 in.
Purchase, The Josephine Bay Paul and C. Michael Paul Foundation, Inc. and the Charles Ulrick and Josephine Bay Foundation, Inc. Gifts, 65.166

This maenad mother, satyr child gently reaching for attention at her side, embodies in her inspired earthiness the personal psychological naturalism in Le Lorrain's style so lauded by his contemporaries. The composition, known from a contemporary engraving, was once thought to have decorated the gardens of Versailles; it represents a movement within the French school toward the informal presentation of classical subjects as artists began to shake off the restraint of the more rigid court style.   JH

Workshop of Andrea del Verrocchio
1435–1488, Italian (Florentine)

Lady with Primroses
Late 15th c.
Plaster, surface stuccoed, polychromed, gilded
H. 25½ in.
Rogers Fund, 65.177

The bust caused rather a stir when it was bought for a small sum at auction. It is a cast of a marble bust in the Bargello in Florence, usually attributed to Verrocchio but sometimes to his famous pupil, Leonardo da Vinci. The Museum did not claim to have bought a Leonardo, but only a copy of a work some scholars have believed to be by him. It has, beyond the subtly graded polychromy, a rare feature in that the copyist included the base, which the original has long since lost.   JDD

Antico (Pier Jacopo Alari-Bonacolsi)
About 1460–1528, Italian (Mantua)

Antoninus Pius
About 1500–1510
Bronze; wreath and mantle gilded
H. 23½ in.
Gift of Edward Fowles, 65.202

Although Antico immersed himself deeply in the imagery and techniques of ancient bronzes, one detects the presence of the quattrocento court goldsmith in the minute workmanship and lyric charm of his style. A close variant is in the Louvre.   JDD

Jean-Baptiste Pigalle

1714–1785, French, after a design by Ange-Jacques Gabriel (1698–1782)

Vase with the attributes of Autumn
(one of a pair)
  About 1745–1747
  Marble
  H. 71 in.
  Purchase, The Josephine Bay Paul and C. Michael Paul Foundation, Inc. and the Charles Ulrick and Josephine Bay Foundation, Inc. Gifts and Rogers Fund, 66.29.1

The Metropolitan's vases were part of a group of four representing Spring and Autumn, originally commissioned for the gardens of the royal Château de Choisy. While derived from antique prototypes, they reflect even more the neoclassical taste of their designer, the king's *premier architecte*. The distinction and appeal of Pigalle's creation lie in the contrast between the picturesque exuberance of its carved paean to nature and the sober framework beneath. The other of the Museum's pair is by Nicolas-Sébastien Adam (1705–1778).   JH

Emile Antoine Bourdelle

1861–1929, French

Mrs. Stephen C. Millett
  About 1921–1925, signed
  Plaster, tinted and polychromed
  H. 20½ in.
  Gift of Stephen C. Millett, 66.42

Bourdelle delved into Coptic funerary portraiture in designing this bust. The subdued polychromy indicates that it was intended for execution in *pâte de verre;* an example of the head alone in that most appealing medium is in the Musée Bourdelle, Paris.   JDD

Auguste Rodin

1840–1917, French

Hand
  About 1886–1889
  Plaster
  L. 3⅛ in.
  Bequest of Malvina C. Hoffman. Presented by Rodin to his pupil Malvina Hoffman and given by her to The Metropolitan Museum of Art, 66.247.4

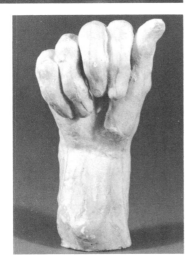

This is one of six Rodin hands in plaster bequeathed to the Museum by his distinguished American pupil. Four are studies associated with his group *The Burghers of Calais,* and this one may have been modeled for the right hand of the burgher Jean d'Aire, who grips an immense key with both hands in the final group.   JDD

Seated nude male figure
  Last quarter of 16th c., Italian
  Bronze
  H. 16 in.
  Edith Perry Chapman Fund, 66.177

A close variant in the museum at Braunschweig is generally attributed to Adrian de Vries, but our example has most often been attributed to Bartolommeo Ammanati, a Florentine sculptor who received part of his training in northern Italy. A distinctly Florentine factor is the pose, derived from Michelangelo's *Battle of Cascina*.   JDD

Guillaume Coustou the Elder
  1677–1746, French

Samuel Bernard
  About 1720
  Marble
  H. 37½ in.
  Purchase, the Josephine Bay Paul and C. Michael Paul Foundation, Inc. and the Charles Ulrick and Josephine Bay Foundation, Inc. Gifts, 66.210

Bernard's canny, determined face, gazing out with pride and some irony from the midst of his heavy court apparel, reminds us of the great financier's rise from humble origins to a position of staggering power as banker to Louis XIV. Dangling across his chest is the coveted order of Saint Michel, presented to him by the king, to the dismay, no doubt, of the old-guard nobility. The combination of baroque bravura and pungent realism is typical of Coustou's finest work.   JH

Pierre-Etienne Monnot
  1657–1733, French

Andromeda Chained to the Rock
  1700–1704, executed in Rome
  Marble
  H. 61 in.
  Purchase, The Josephine Bay Paul and C. Michael Paul Foundation, Inc. and the Charles Ulrick and Josephine Bay Foundation, Inc. Gifts 67.34

When John Cecil, Earl of Exeter, commissioned a series of sculptures in Rome, his choice fell not on an Italian but on one of the French artists who dominated the field of Roman monumental sculpture at the time. This coolly poised work, with its brilliant carving and psychological dissolution of spatial bounds, is a vivid example of the late baroque in Rome.   JH

Luca della Robbia
1399/1400–1482, Italian (Florentine)

Virgin and Child in niche
Mid-15th c.
Glazed terracotta
H. 19 in.
Bequest of Susan Dwight Bliss, 67.55.98

An unusually precious work by Luca, founder of the della Robbia dynasty of sculptors, this is distinguished for its modeling and its progressive note of illusionism, the group conceived as if viewed through the niche enframement. Moreover, there is a superb ornamental interaction among the white figures, the clear blue of the niche, and its rare gilt details.   JDD

Cupid Blindfolded
Mid-16th c., south German
Bronze
H. 8¾ in.
Bequest of Susan Dwight Bliss, 67.55.99

Probably a fountain figure. While exaggeratedly fat, it has a sophisticated serpentine movement. A perfect example of a model otherwise known only in a flawed bronze in Berlin.   JDD

Antonio Canova
1757–1822, Italian

Perseus
1804–1806
Marble
H. 86⅝ in.
Fletcher Fund, 67.110

Canova was the genius of neoclassicism in sculpture. Consistent with his worldwide fame, his heroic composition of *Perseus* in the Vatican Museum, finished in 1801, was repeated in this example for a Polish countess, Valeria Tarnowska. The Museum owns the original contract, dated 1804, as well as two heads of the slain Medusa, one in plaster and a hollow one in marble. Canova explained to his patroness why he was providing two heads: the plaster one would add less weight to the outstretched arm, while the countess could amuse herself by putting a candle in the marble one and watching the eerie play of light.   JDD

Aristide Maillol
1861–1944, French

Summer
First modeled 1910–1911, signed
Bronze
H. 63½ in.
Bequest of Miss Adelaide Milton de Groot
(1876–1967), 67.187.46

The model was commissioned by the Russian collector Morosoff. A bronze of it in the Pushkin Museum in Moscow joins three others collectively called The Seasons. The subject, however, is not the main point. André Gide wrote of another of Maillol's monumental nudes: "She is beautiful. She has no meaning. This is a work of silence."   JDD

Jean-Louis Lemoyne
1665–1755, French

The Fear of Cupid's Darts
1739–1740
Marble
H. 72 in.
Purchase, The Josephine Bay Paul and C.
    Michael Paul Foundation, Inc. and the
    Charles Ulrick and Josephine Bay Founda-
    tion, Inc. Gifts, 67.197

This playfully erotic portrayal of a young nymph, at once fearful and fascinated at the approach of love, reflects the lingering mood of the *Régence*. However, its evanescent surfaces and delicately off-balance pose, all entirely rococo, as well as the psychological precision of the nymph's gesture and expression, make it seem likely that Lemoyne's son, Jean-Baptiste, had a hand in the execution.   JH

Giovanni Caccini
1556–1612, Italian (Florence)

Temperance
1583–1584
Marble
H. 72 in.
Harris Brisbane Dick Fund, 67.208

The figure holds mathematical instruments, signifying measured reason, and the bridle of restraint. Caccini was an associate of Giovanni Bologna and followed his master closely in the fluency and modulation of gesture and stance, but the thick bands of drapery are a personal idiosyncracy of Caccini's. Borghini's *Riposo* of 1584 mentioned that the work was in progress for the garden of the palace of Giovanni Battista del Milanese, Bishop of Marsica, in via Larga, Florence.   JDD

Jean-Baptiste Carpeaux
1827–1875, French

Ugolino and His Sons
1865–1867, signed
Saint-Béat marble
H. 77 in.
Purchase, The Josephine Bay Paul and C. Michael Paul Foundation, Inc. and the Charles Ulrick and Josephine Bay Foundation, Inc. Gifts, 67.250

The story of the imprisonment and starvation of the Pisan traitor Count Ugolino della Gherardesca, with his sons and grandsons, is told in *The Divine Comedy*. Carpeaux was obsessed with Dante's horrific tale, and his titanic Michelangelesque figures were years in the making. A bronze shown in the Salon of 1863 is now in the Louvre. This marble group was realized at the behest of M. Dervillé, proprietor of the Saint-Béat marble quarries, and shown at the *Exposition Universelle* of 1867.   JDD

Sleeping Hercules
About 1500, north Italian
Bronze
H. 5⅜ in.
Gift of Irwin Untermyer, 68.141.18

The unusual subject as well as some uncertainties about authorship give added interest to this outstanding bronze. The harmonious composition and finely hammered surfaces show a master in total command of his medium.   JDD

Juan de Ancheta
About 1540–1592, Spanish

Saint John the Baptist
About 1580–1592, school of Navarre
Wood relief, polychromed and gilded
H. 44¼ in.
Rogers Fund. 68.173

Illustrative of the Spanish technique *estofado* (painting and tooling on a gold-brushed panel), the relief was identified by Olga Raggio as a work of Juan de Ancheta. It no doubt formed part of a *retablo,* the characteristic form of Spanish altarpiece containing many painted and gilt panels.   JDD

Melchiorre Caffà

1630/1635–1667, Italian (Rome)

Bishop Saint
About 1650–1667
Terracotta model
H. 14¼ in.
Gift of William B. Jaffe, 68.218

The figure has a nobility of stance and a vivacity of modeling that recall Bernini, particularly his saints for the Cathedra Petri in St. Peter's (1657–1666). Such models, beyond their prior function as preparatory designs, were treasured properties in a Roman atelier, where they served as teaching devices, showing the ideas of the master in their freshest state.   JDD

Lazzaro Casario

Died about 1593, Italian (Bologna)

Elisabetta Bianchini Vizzani
Dated 1589, inscribed with names of sculptor and subject
Marble
H. 31 in.
Harris Brisbane Dick Fund, 69.48

The sculptor has distilled the somber essences of the Counter Reformation in his very realistic image of a widow. The effigy was no doubt carved for the Vizzani family chapel in S. Giovanni in Monte, Bologna.   JDD

Jean-Baptiste Stouf

1742–1826, French

André-Ernest-Modeste Grétry
1804–1809
Marble
H. 68 in.
Purchase, The Josephine Bay Paul and C. Michael Paul Foundation, Inc. and the Charles Ulrick and Josephine Bay Foundation, Inc. Gifts, 69.77

The composer is attired in his dressing gown, leaning against a column inscribed with the names of forty-one of his operas. Stouf's neoclassical monument was placed in the foyer of the Opéra-Comique in Paris within Grétry's lifetime, a sign of the celebrity the composer enjoyed.   JDD

Infant Blowing a Conch Shell
  About 1670–1680, French, probably executed
    for one of the *bosquets* in the gardens of
    Versailles
  Lead
  H. 23 in.
  Purchase, The Josephine Bay Paul and C.
    Michael Paul Foundation, Inc. and the
    Charles Ulrick and Josephine Bay Founda-
    tion, Inc. Gifts, 69.78

This vigorous marine child must be imagined
emerging from a pool, a spray of water pluming
from his shell; he exemplifies the sort of charming
conceits designed by Charles Le Brun to enliven
the gardens at Versailles.   JH

Johann Heinrich Dannecker
  1758–1841, German (Stuttgart)

The Muse of History
  About 1789
  Terracotta
  H. 29 in.
  Gift of Paul E. Manheim, 69.288

Dannecker evolved a weighty, very distinguished
style of neoclassicism after training in Paris and
Rome. Comparisons with standing figures of
Tragedy and History in a relief of 1789 and a
seated *Girl with a Bird* of 1790 make it likely that
Dannecker modeled our statuette in Rome or soon
after his return to Stuttgart in 1789.   JDD

Michel Anguier
  1612/14–1686, French

Leda and the Swan
  Dated 1654
  Limestone
  H. 86 in.
  Purchase, The Josephine Bay Paul and C.
    Michael Paul Foundation, Inc. and the
    Charles Ulrick and Josephine Bay Founda-
    tion, Inc. Gifts and Rogers Fund, 1970.140

Thought to have been made for the château of
Saint-Mandé, a property of the finance minister
Nicolas Foucquet, this contains both the delicacy
and the robustness that characterize French classicism in sculpture before the Louis XIV style
emerged. The inscription on the front of the base
is relatively modern.   JDD

Antonio Canova
1757–1822, Italian

Reclining Naiad
   Commissioned in or about 1819; completed in
     or about 1824
   Marble
   L. 75 in.
   Purchase, Mrs. Joseph A. Neff Gift in memory
     of Joseph A. Neff, 1970.1

The reclining female nude was a favorite subject in the art of Canova, his best known being *Pauline Borghese* in the Borghese Gallery, Rome. The first marble *Naiad,* now at Buckingham Palace, was created for Lord Cawdor between 1815 and 1817. Our second version, made for Lord Darnley's country estate, was completed by studio assistants after Canova's death.   JDD

The Mourning Virgin
   About 1700, south German
   Wood, polychromed and gilded
   H. 38¼ in.
   Harris Brisbane Dick Fund, 1971.15

The figure is to be understood as part of a typical Crucifixion group of the Virgin and Saint John flanking the crucified Christ. The brilliant flame-like movement is a sign of the reviving Gothic. A taste for the Gothic never died out completely in Germany and it revisited the late baroque with a vengeance.   JDD

Fortuna
   About 1560–1570, Italian (Florence)
   Bronze
   H. 21¼ in.
   Edith Perry Chapman Fund, 1970.57

The vigorous, serpentine modeling and precise, assured tooling suggest that the bronze was cast (though never completely finished) in Florence soon after the execution of the model, which has been traditionally ascribed to the Venetian Danese Cattaneo, though it cannot lie far from early work by Giovanni Bologna (1529–1608). Only the ends of the semicircular sail of Fortuna (intact in some later examples) remain in the figure's hands.   JDD

Jean-Baptiste Carpeaux
1827–1875, French

The Genius of the Dance
1872, signed
Bronze model
H. 22⅞ in.
Rogers fund, 1970.171

A reduction of the central figure of Carpeaux's famous, controversial group of *The Dance,* made 1865–1869 for the façade of the Paris Opéra. The highly idealized head combines that of the Raphael *Saint Michael* and that of Empress Eugénie, who became a standard of beauty for Carpeaux. The statuette, with its characteristic crosshatched chasing, has not only textural but technical interest; its joining seams and connecting rods indicate it was the model from which finished bronzes in this scale were produced. It was sold together with the rights of reproduction in the sale of Carpeaux's atelier in 1894.   JDD

Tiziano Aspetti
1565–1607, Italian (Padua)

Scenes from the Martyrdom of Saint Daniel of Padua
Commissioned 1592
Bronze reliefs
19 x 29¼ in.
Edith Perry Chapman and Fletcher Funds, 1970.264.1,2

The Counter Reformation in Italy saw an increase in the literal depiction of the martyrdom of saints. Here, the appalling spectacles of Saint Daniel being dragged by a horse and then nailed between a table of wood and one of stone are presented with the full repertory of classical and Renaissance poses and gestures, richly varied. These reliefs formerly ornamented the altar of the saint in the Cathedral of Padua.   JDD

Saint Joseph and the Christ Child
   Second half of 17th c., Netherlandish
   Boxwood
   H. 10 11/16 in.
   Rogers Fund, 1971.68

The suave little group is representative of the pietistic scenes from the daily life of the Holy Family that were produced in abundance in the seventeenth century. The child in particular has a Rubensian vigor.   JDD

Simone Mosca
   1492–1553, Italian

Wall fountain
   Florentine, erected in Arezzo about 1528
   Gray sandstone
   H. about 16 ft. 3 in.
   Harris Brisbane Dick Fund, 1971.158

A master of stately High Renaissance ornament, Mosca made this fountain and a fireplace for Palazzo Fossombroni in Arezzo, where both were seen and praised by his fellow Aretine, Giorgio Vasari. The fireplace is in the Museo Civico at Arezzo.   JDD

Louis-Claude Vassé
   1716–1772, French

Wall fountain with Nymph Drying Her Hair
   Dated 1763, signed
   Marble and gilt-bronze
   H. fountain 102½ in.
   Purchase, The Josephine Bay Paul and C. Michael Paul Foundation, Inc. and the Charles Ulrick and Josephine Bay Foundation, Inc. Gifts and Rogers Fund, 1971.205

The aquatic imagery is playful, with the nymph wringing her hair and the bronze serpents spitting water into the basin, but the coolly poised figure itself, derived from an ancient Venus, and the refined ornament of the basin are sure signs of neoclassicism stirring within the prevailing rococo trend. The plaster model was shown at the Salon of 1761, where the catalogue stated that it was to be executed in marble for the Duc de Chevreuse at Dampierre.   JDD

Day and Dusk
After sculptures by Michelangelo Buonarroti (1475–1564) in the Medici Chapel, Church of San Lorenzo, Florence
Terracotta
H. 16, 15 in.
Gift of Charles Wrightsman, 1971.206.35,36

The origin of these, as of the numerous other reduced versions of Michelangelo's brooding personifications on the Medici tombs, is a vexed issue. The style of this pair differs markedly from Michelangelo's own; the careful surfaces and precise, formalized delineation of the musculature and hair suggest a late mannerist Florentine source, but an eighteenth-century origin in the north has also been proposed.   JH

Auguste Préault
1809–1879, French

The Actor Rouvière as Hamlet Recoiling before the Ghost
Dated 1866
Signature effaced and replaced by that of Dalou (spurious)
20½ x 24¼ in.
Rogers Fund, 1972.2

Préault was possessed of an overwhelming romantic imagination evident in the dramatic contrast between the agitated Hamlet and the chill ghost in shallower relief.   JDD

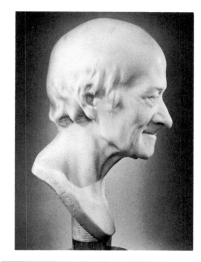

Jean-Antoine Houdon
1741–1828, French

Voltaire
Dated 1778, signed
Marble
H. 18⅞ in.
Purchase, Charles Wrightsman Gift, 1972.61

This gripping image of the great man in his last
year was produced, like Houdon's *Diderot* bust,
1974.291, for Count Stroganoff. For a century and
a half the two formed pendants in the Stroganoff
Palace in St. Petersburg.   JDD

Pope Saint Pius V
Possibly after a model by Camillo Rusconi
(1658–1728)
Early 18th c., Italian (Rome)
Gilt-bronze in relief on an ornamental bracket
H. 25½ in.
Ann and George Blumenthal Fund, 1972.86

Pius V (reigned 1566–1572) was beatified in 1672
and canonized in 1712. His ascetic features are
here set off by the undulating surfaces of the gilt
relief, a late baroque creation probably dating
from the reign of Clement XI, when there was a
renewed devotion to the saint's cult.   JDD

Bertel Thorvaldsen
About 1770–1844, Danish

Christian Charity
About 1808, modeled in Rome
Terracotta relief
H. 26 in.
Purchase, Irwin Untermyer Gift and Rogers
Fund, 1973.81

Thorvaldsen was the dominant neoclassical
sculptor after Canova. This grave little procession
was repeated in two marble reliefs with slight
variations, one appropriately enough for an alms
box in the Metropolitan Church of Our Lady,
Copenhagen.   JDD

Neptune
   About 1700, probably Flemish
   Terracotta
   H. 13⅛ in.
   Gift of Joseph F. McCrindle, 1973.184.1

This and a pendant *River God* (1973.184.2) are models, probably for much larger garden figures. They are amusingly distorted imitations of types current in French baroque classicism, in the manner of Girardon and Coysevox but gone quite awry.   JDD

Robert Le Lorrain
   1666–1743, French

Dancing Bacchante
   Early 18th c.
   Bronze mounted on ebony and gilt-bronze base
   H. figure 12⅝ in.
   Rogers Fund, 1973.263

The earnest overtones of Le Lorrain's lead *Bacchante and Young Satyr* are absent from this intimate collector's version of the single figure, a bronze example of which was shown by the artist at the Salon of 1704. In contrast to the ponderous lurching movement of the garden sculpture, the warmly patinated bronze is characterized by an ethereal contrapposto and lightness of limb.   JH

Ecce Homo
   Late 16th-early 17th c., Flemish or Dutch
   Silver and silver-gilt relief in ebony and rose-
      wood frame with silver and silver-gilt appli-
      ques and cartouche
   13½ x 11½ in. (with frame)
   Ann and George Blumenthal Fund, 1973.286

This scene may have an as yet undiscovered engraved source. Full of picturesque touches such as are met with in the work of Lucas van Leyden, the relief has a different spirit from the decorative reliefs on the frame, which are in the lobate style of the Utrecht goldsmith Paulus van Vianen and his followers. The arms of Pope Alexander VII at the bottom were added later. A letter in a seventeenth-century hand, affixed to the back, states that Alexander conferred an indulgence on the relief.   JDD

Workshop of Alessandro Leopardi
Active from 1482—died 1522/23, Italian (Venetian)

Pricket candlesticks with reliefs of Saints Peter and Paul
About 1510
Bronze, partially gilded
H. 36, 36½ in.
Ann and George Blumenthal Fund, 1973.287.1,2

Analogies of texture and composition (figures from which a Byzantine stiffness has not altogether disappeared) between these and three flagpole stands by Alessandro Leopardi in Piazza S. Marco, Venice, permit an attribution of the candlesticks at least to Leopardi's sphere of influence. The candlesticks were part of a set of six for an altar. Two with reliefs of Saints Matthew and Luke are in the Pierpont Morgan Library, and two with Saints Mark and John are in the Victoria and Albert Museum. JDD

Alessandro Algardi
1598–1654, Italian (Bologna, active in Rome)

Pair of firedogs: Jupiter Victorious over the Titans, Juno Controlling the Winds
Second half of 17th c., probably cast in Rome
Bronze
H. 45½ in.
Gift of Charles Wrightsman, 1973.315.16,17

In the last year of his life, Algardi modeled firedogs with these subjects for the king of Spain. Theatrical baroque furnishings, they were repeated several times in silver as well as bronze for the European courts and nobility. The taut, superb facture of the present casts indicates a Roman foundry. JDD

Jean-Jacques Caffiéri
1725–1792, French

Claude-Adrien Helvétius
Dated 1772, signed
Terracotta
H. 18⅝ in.
Gift of Charles Wrightsman, 1973.315.19

A sensitive model, with autograph touches visible in the clay throughout, for a marble bust in the Louvre, also dated 1772. The marble was ordered by Mme. Helvétius as a remembrance of her *philosophe*-husband, who died in 1771.   JDD

Bertoldo di Giovanni
Died 1491, Italian (Florentine)
Filippo de' Medici, Archbishop of Pisa (Reverse: *The Last Judgment*)
About 1474
Bronze medal
D. 2 3/16 in.
Rogers Fund, 1974.166

Filippo de' Medici, a distant relation of Lorenzo the Magnificent, was Archbishop of Pisa from 1462 until his death in 1474. The portrait is the most sensitive among those by Bertoldo, an intimate of Lorenzo. The beautiful reverse has been said, surprisingly but accurately, to have influenced Michelangelo's preliminary designs for his fresco in the Sistine Chapel.   JDD

John Henry Foley
1818–1874, Irish (active in England)

A Youth at a Stream
Dated 1844, signed
Lead
H. 21½ in.
Fanny Shapiro Bequest and Rogers Fund,
1974.196

A lacquer patination was added to give the look of bronze to this reduction of a model exhibited at Westminster Hall in 1844. The subject matter has not been accounted for, except that it is known to illustrate these lines: "Playful and wanton to the stream he trips,/And dips his foot."

JDD

Joseph Nollekens
1737–1823, English

William Pitt
Dated 1807, signed
Marble
H. 23½ in.
Gift of Mrs. Francis Henry Lenygon, 1974.209

Although it is said that Nollekens sold some seventy-four examples of his posthumous bust of Pitt, this example is worked so incisively as to suggest that it had at least some share of the artist's attention. Surprisingly, it is the first English bust of the period to enter our collections.

JDD

Jean-Antoine Houdon
1741–1828, French

Diderot
Dated 1773, signed
Marble
H. 20 7/16 in.
Gift of Charles Wrightsman, 1974.291

With its slightly nervous sideward movement, the bust embodies the questing intellect of the encyclopedist. An almost identical marble in the Hermitage was made for Catherine II of Russia; ours was executed for Count Alexander Sergeivitch Stroganoff, like Catherine an admirer of Diderot and all things French.

JDD

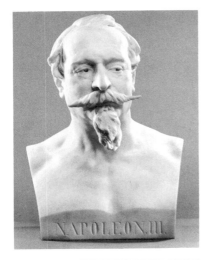

Jean-Baptiste Carpeaux
1827–1875, French

Napoleon III
  Dated 1873, signed
  Marble, H. 20½ in.
  Purchase, Ann and George Blumenthal Fund,
    Munsey and Fletcher Funds, funds from var-
    ious donors, Agnes Shewan Rizzo Bequest,
    and Mrs. Peter Oliver Gift, 1974.297

Napoleon III died in exile at Chiselhurst in 1873.
The imperial family summoned the great romantic
realist Carpeaux to England, where he recorded
the emperor's features in death. Afterward, he
produced this first example of the marble bust
entirely by his own hand. An intensely searching
and partisan souvenir of the fallen leader's trou-
bled but majestic countenance, it was owned by
the widowed empress Eugénie until her death
nearly half a century later.   JDD

Vincenzo Gemito
1852–1929, Italian (Naples)

The Painter Meissonier
  Modeled in Paris, 1878/79, signed
  Bronze
  H. 21⅞ in.
  Edith Perry Chapman Fund, 1975.26

The celebrated concocter of battle scenes is
observed as if standing before his easel. Potbelly
and all, his stance is a spectacularly balanced
network of triangulations.   JDD

Model for an altar
  First half of 18th c., Italian
  Terracotta
  H. 8¼ in.
  Gift of Ruth Blumka in memory of Leopold
    Blumka, 1975.73

The model has alternate suggestions for the com-
pletion of the sides and the surmounting tabernacle. It is rather similar in style to some architectural drawings by Luigi Vanvitelli (1700–1773).
                                                JDD

Attributed to Giles Grendey
1693–1780, English

Armchair
About 1740
Mahogany, partially gilded
H. 42½ in.
Gift of Irwin Untermyer, 64.101.964

The lions' heads and paws that give imposing character to chairs of the early Georgian period are here enlivened by the gilding of other decorative carving. There is a comparable chair in Longford Castle, Wiltshire, where records of payments to "Greenday chairmaker" still exist. PH

Armchair
About 1755, English
Mahogany
H. 51 in.
Gift of Irwin Untermyer, 64.101.980

In Chippendale's designs, chairs in the style of this particularly extravagant example were dubbed "French," although they far exceed their models in erratic contour and multiplication of carved ornament. PH

Long table
About 1620, English
Oak
L. 128 in.
Gift of Irwin Untermyer, 64.101.1065

The term "refectory table" derives from a mistaken idea that such tables were used by monks in the refectories of monasteries, all of which had been suppressed in England by 1540. A more proper name, "long table," occurs in country house inventories of the Elizabethan and Jacobean periods. The bulbous legs, resembling contemporary silver covered cups, are of Flemish origin, and bear witness to the international circulation of engraved ornament designs and the immigration of Protestant craftsmen from the Continent. JP

Secretary bookcase
  About 1740, English
  Walnut, carved and gilded limewood
  H. 82½ in.
  Gift of Irwin Untermyer, 64.101.1110

The star piece in the collection formed early in this century by the noted English connoisseur of furniture, Percival Griffiths, this was later acquired by an equally distinguished American collector, Judge Irwin Untermyer.   JP

Court cupboard
  About 1585, English
  Oak, walnut
  H. 48½ in.
  Gift of Irwin Untermyer, 64.101.1134

Such short ("court") pieces of furniture were made to display the wealth of their owners in the form of silver vessels ("cups"), visibly stored on each of the three tiers ("boards").   PH

Commode
  About 1775, English
  Satinwood, mahogany, gilt-bronze, *giallo antico* marble top
  H. 38 in.
  Gift of Irwin Untermyer, 64.101.1145

The gilt-bronze rams have been attributed to Matthew Boulton, the one English manufacturer of decorative hardware to escape the anonymity of his colleagues, who lacked guild records to perpetuate their names. Boulton, with his partner John Fothergill, was responsible for an assembly-line production, 1768–1782, covering categories from buttons to vases, on a scale so comprehensive that Josiah Wedgwood deemed him "the most complete manufacturer in England of metal."   PH

Robert Adam (designer)
  1728–1792, English

Sefferin Alken (carver)
  Died 1783

Side table
  1765, Croome Court, Worcestershire
  Painted deal, marble
  H. 35½ in.
  Fletcher Fund, 65.127

The Philadelphia Museum owned this and an identical table; the Metropolitan owned the two mirrors made to hang over them. An exchange was effected to provide each museum with a table and mirror. Carved festoons of husks, now missing, originally linked the table's front and side legs.   PH

Desk cabinet
  About 1760, English (Holme Lacy, Hereford-
    shire)
  Mahogany
  H. 92 in.
  Bequest of Bernard M. Baruch, 65.155.24

The popularity of such fanciful concoctions inspired the architect Sir William Chambers to
publish in 1757 a book of designs conscientiously
observed on a journey to China, in the stated
hope that it "might be of use in putting a stop
to the extravagancies that daily appear under the
name of Chinese."   PH

Paneling from an Elizabethan room
  About 1600, English (Star Hotel, Great
    Yarmouth, Norfolk)
  Oak
  L. 23 ft. 6 in., W. 21 ft. 10½ in., H. 11 ft.
  Edward Pearce Casey Fund, 65.182.1

This elaborate specimen of late Tudor wood
carving was the principal apartment of the residence built by William Crowe, a merchant ad-
venturer of the sort that flourished during the
reign of Queen Elizabeth. He must have been as
proud of his profession as he was successful in
it, for he had the arms of the company of Spanish
merchants to which he belonged carved over his
mantel. The house was operated as an inn from
the eighteenth century until its demolition in
1935.   PH

Bed
  Second half of 15th c., Italian (Florence)
  Walnut
  L. with dais 102⅞ in.
  Gift of George R. Hann, 65.221.1

This multifunctional survival from Renaissance
Florence would have been the only piece required
to furnish a room. The dais surrounding the bed
served as a seating unit, hinged for access to
storage compartments below.   PH

Attributed to Christopher Fuhrlohg

Commode
  About 1772, English
  Mahogany, deal, satinwood, harewood, tulip-
    wood, lacquered bronze
  H. 37¾ in.
  From the Marion E. and Leonard A. Cohn Col-
    lection, 66.64.2

Fuhrlohg, a Swede, was apprenticed in Stock-
holm and worked in Paris before establishing
himself in London as a specialist in marquetry
furniture in the French manner. This piece is an
idiosyncratic adaptation of the French transition
between rococo and neoclassic models.   PH

Desk
  About 1790, English
  Yewwood, walnut, satinwood, other woods,
    gilt-bronze
  H. 41 5/16 in.
  From the Marion E. and Leonard A. Cohn Col-
    lection, 66.64.5

The idea for this type, with a raised partition in
the back, was conceived in France about 1750.
Extensively used by lady letterwriters, it received
the coquettish name *bonheur-du-jour*. The plain,
elegant lines of this example are set off by exceptionally fine, characteristically English marquetry.   JP

Pair of candlestands
  About 1755–1760, English
  Mahogany
  H. 51½ in.
  From the Marion E. and Leonard A. Cohn Col-
    lection, 66.64.9,10

Chinese fretwork first appeared in England early
in the eighteenth century in garden fences, but it
was not until mid-century that the vogue for
fretwork on furniture erupted. The model of these
candlestands is Plate CXX in the first edition of
Thomas Chippendale's *Gentleman and Cabinet-
Maker's Director (1754)*.   PH

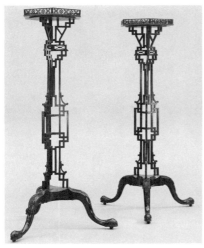

Pair of armchairs
  About 1780, Italian (Naples)
  Walnut, polychromed
  H. 35¾ in.
  Gift of Sarah Hunter Kelly, 66.237.1,2

These supplement another pair and a settee from the same set acquired in 1926. Characteristically Italian is the lightheartedness of the design of fluttering birds attempting to uplift the gaily painted chair frames.   PH

Armchair and side chair
  1811–1820, English
  Mahogany covered in leopard skin
  H. 43¾, 36 1/16 in.
  Rogers Fund, 67.63.1,2

The *klismos,* with splayed legs and round back, was an antique form resuscitated in the archaeological enthusiasm of the late eighteenth century. The signature "C. Dixwell 1820" beneath the seat rail of the side chair is that of Charles Dixwell, a London "upholder," a profession including the tasks of upholsterer, furniture repairman, and undertaker.   PH

Art nouveau room
  1910–1914, French
  Paintings and designs by Lucien Lévy-Dhurmer,
    1865–1953
  Woodwork executed by Edward Louis Collet,
    1876–
  Walnut, purple wood, various other materials
  Harris Brisbane Dick Fund, 66.244.1–26

The 1973 exhibition at the Grand Palais in Paris announced the rediscovery of Lucien Lévy-Dhurmer and his circle. Seven years earlier the Metropolitan had been able to acquire this room, complete with its original contents, representing the most comprehensive creation of his gentle genius. For the dining room of his friend Albert Rateau, Lévy-Dhurmer painted scenes of a wisteria-filled garden and designed the paneling, furniture, lighting fixtures, and carpet.   PH

Martin Carlin
  Died 1785, master 1766. French

Bookcase
  About 1785
  Tulipwood, satiné, oak, gilt-bronze
  H. 80 in.
  Bequest of Mary Hayward Weir, 69.9.2

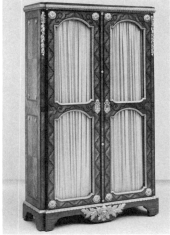

Carlin worked primarily for *marchands-merciers,* the decorator-dealers who guided Parisian fashion, and he knew well how to finesse elegance. Given the task of constructing a bookcase of sizable mass, he created an effect of airy lightness by the use of delicate marquetry, glittering gilt-bronze and, above all, skillful design.   PH

Pair of bookcases
  Late 17th–early 18th c., Italian (Rome)
  Walnut, poplar
  H. 13 ft. 3 in.
  Gift of Madame Lilliana Teruzzi, 69.292.1,2

Although architects' drawings of the seventeenth and eighteenth centuries show wire-mesh-fronted bookcases built into the wood paneling of libraries, this pair, recorded in the 1722 inventory of the Palazzo Rospigliosi, were designed as independent monumental structures.   PH

Giuseppe Maria Bonzanigo
1745–1820, Italian (Turin)

Console table
1782–1792
Poplar, painted and gilded
H. 36 1/2 in.
Rogers Fund, by exchange, 1970.4

A tour de force of lapidary wood carving, this table can be compared only with other works supplied by Bonzanigo to Victor Amadeus III, king of Savoy. Although he based the cameo scene of Leda on a 1782 engraving by Michelangelo Pergolesi, none but the master carver himself would have dared design the implausibly delicate openwork legs.   PH

Harpsichord and stool
   Late 17th c., Italian (Rome)
   Elm and birch, partially gilded and painted
   H. with top raised 66½ in.
   Gift of Madame Lilliana Teruzzi, 1971.4.1,2

Designed to be the focus of visual as well as auditory attention during a musical performance. The exterior is elaborately carved and gilded; the interiors of the lid and keyboard-cover are painted with landscapes attributed to the artist Crescenzio Onofri (1632–1698).   PH

Jacob Frères
   Georges II Jacob, 1768–1803, and François-
      Honoré-Georges Jacob (called Jacob-Desmal-
      ter), 1770–1841, French

Daybed
1795–1803
Mahogany, beech, gilt-bronze
L. 76¾ in.
Gift of Charles Wrightsman, 1971.206.13

A succession of notable ladies including Caroline Murat, Pauline Borghese (sister of Napoleon), and the Duchesse d'Angoulême (daughter of Louis XVI) must have reclined on this. The inventory marks it bears show that it traveled from the château of Neuilly to the Trianon, the Tuileries, and the château of Villeneuve l'Etang before it returned to the Murat family and was sold at auction in 1961 by the heirs of Princesse Cécile-Caroline Murat.   PH

Georges Jacob

1739–1814, master 1765, French

Firescreen
>About 1786
>Beechwood, gilded with traces of silvering;
>   panel: contemporary silk brocade
>H. 42 in.
>Gift of Charles Wrightsman, 1971.206.16

Jacob carved this screen and the set of chairs
made with it to accord with the existing furnishings of Marie Antoinette's boudoir at Fontainebleau, repeating the molding of spiraling ribbon
and pearls on her desk and wall paneling, and
the cupid's bow and flower garland of the man-
telpiece decoration. The presence of Saint-Cloud
inventory marks indicates that the screen later
formed part of the furnishings of that château.
                                                      PH

Guillaume Beneman

Master 1785, French

Secretary
>Caryatid figures modeled by Louis-Simon
>   Boizot, 1743–1809
>1786–87
>Oak, tulipwood, kingwood, holly, gilt-bronze
>H. 63½ in.
>Gift of Charles Wrightsman, 1971.206.17

Along with a commode and writing table, this
secretary was commissioned for the Cabinet
Intérieur of Louis XVI at the palace of Compiègne,
to go with one of three commodes provided as
furnishings for Marie Antoinette when she married the dauphin, and discarded by her as out of
style in 1786. In an economy measure typical of
the regime, Louis XVI absorbed them into his own
apartments, going to great expense to refurbish
them and have complementary pieces made with
equally lavish gilt-bronze decoration.   PH

Charles Cressent (casemaker)

1686–1768, French

Jean Godde l'aîné (movement)

Wall clock
>About 1733
>Gilt-bronze, brass
>H. 52½ in.
>Gift of Charles Wrightsman, 1971.206.27

The duality of talent and interest inherited by
Charles Cressent, whose father was a sculptor
and whose grandfather was a cabinetmaker, is

responsible for much of the documentation we have on his work. Evidence of his violation of guild regulations prohibiting casting and gilding of bronze in a cabinetmaker's workshop, presented in a 1733 lawsuit, included the description of a similar clock, depicting the Triumph of Love over Time, which Cressent was in the course of making for King John V of Portugal.   PH

Pair of wall lights
    1745–1749, French
    Gilt-bronze
    H. 30½ in.
    Gift of Charles Wrightsman, 1971.206.30

The high rococo asymmetry of the swirling branches is datable by the presence of the crowned *C* stamp. The mark was affixed upon payment of a tax levied on gilt-bronze 1745–1749.
                                                PH

Mounts attributed to Pierre-Philippe Thomire
    1751–1843, French
Vase and column
    About 1773
    Porphyry, gilt-bronze
    H. vase 39½ in., column 41 in.
    Gift of Charles Wrightsman, 1971.206.44

The single column from which this vase and pedestal were cut was probably quarried by the Romans in Egypt. In the wave of neoclassicism, such columns were stripped from Roman ruins and brought to France to be refashioned in the royal stone-cutting and polishing workshop established in Paris about 1772.   PH

Showcase on stand
    Late 17th c., Italian (Rome)
    Walnut, gilded lindenwood, glass
    H. 7 ft. 7 in.
    Gift of Madame Lilliana Teruzzi, 1972.73

A kneeling bearded man holds aloft a vitrine, and four lively children ride atop, around the enframed head of a full-faced beauty. The piece exemplifies the theatrical impact of sculptural Italian furniture.   PH

Room from the Hôtel de Cabris
  About 1775, French
  Oak, painted and gilded
  L. 24 ft. 5½ in., W. 19 ft. 5¾ in., H. 11 ft. 7½ in.
  Charles Wrightsman Gift, 1972.276.1

This latest addition to the adjoining period rooms given by Mr. and Mrs. Charles Wrightsman was made in Paris for the Hôtel de Cabris, now the Musée Fragonard, in Grasse. The hôtel was completed in 1774, but this wall paneling, for the "salon de compagnie," remained in crates until the nineteenth century.   PH

Gilles Joubert
  1689–1775, French

Writing table
  1759
  Oak with red japanning, gilt-bronze
  H. 31¾ in.
  Gift of Charles Wrightsman, 1973.315.1

The epitome of rococo furniture, fusing color, shape, and decoration, documented by the number 2131 painted underneath. Under that number in the Journal du Garde-Meuble, the royal furniture registry, is the record of its delivery by Joubert on December 29, 1759, for use by Louis XV in the Cabinet Intérieur, his favorite study at Versailles.   PH

Pair of candelabra
  About 1790, French
  Red griotte, gray bardiglio marble, gilt-bronze
  H. 47 3/8 in.
  Gift of Charles Wrightsman, 1973.315.4,5

The ultimate extravaganza of the bronze worker's repertory, these stand on two tiers of animal feet, the stem topped by female terms, the branches adorned with grape vines, eagle heads, snakes, and ending in jesters' heads supporting tambourines that catch the candlewax.   PH

Commode
>About 1765, German (Bamberg)
>
>Pine, carved and gilded on white painted ground, red *rance* marble top
>
>H. 32½ in.
>
>Bequest of Emma A. Sheafer, The Lesley and Emma Sheafer Collection, 1974.356.129

The undulating lines of the front and sides suggest that its creator had seen the swell-fronted painted or laquered commodes made in Venice in the mid-eighteenth century. The carved motifs are thought to have been carried out in the studio of Ferdinand Tietz (1708–1777). He is known to have provided large stone figures for the gardens of Seehof Castle, whence came this piece.   JP

Console table
>About 1765, German (Bamberg)
>
>Limewood, carved and gilded, Sarrancolin marble top
>
>H. 32¾ in.
>
>Bequest of Emma A. Sheafer, The Lesley and Emma Sheafer Collection, 1974.356.127

The motifs at the tops of the legs symbolize the Seasons (here, a dragon at the left, emblematic of Summer, and the head of the wind-god Boreas at the right for Spring). The pair is thought to be among the many commissions carried out for Prince-Bishop Adam Friedrich von Seinsheim by the sculptor and woodcarver Ferdinand Tietz.
                                                    JP

Card table
>About 1750, German (Bamberg)
>
>Walnut, carved, top veneered with marquetry woods
>
>H. 29½ in.
>
>Bequest of Emma A. Sheafer, The Lesley and Emma Sheafer Collection, 1974.356.126

According to the Bamberg city archives, Nicolaus Bauer (active 1758–1771) made gaming tables for Seehof Castle, the summer residence of the bishops of Würzburg and Bamberg, during the 1750s and 60s. This example, coming from Seehof, can be included in his output. The folding top exhibits marquetry motifs typical of German workshops, while carved asymmetrical shellwork elements adorn the knees.   JP

Commode
  About 1740–1750, German (Munich)
  Pine, carved, painted, gilded, marbelized wood
    top
  H. 33 in.
  Bequest of Emma A. Sheafer, The Lesley and
    Emma Sheafer Collection, 1974.356.97

The decoration, gilded carving on a milky white ground, would have corresponded closely with the carved woodwork décor of the room in which it stood, for such commodes, like console tables, were made to complement their surroundings. A French-trained architect, François de Cuvilliès (1695–1768) provided designs of similar commodes intended for Bavarian rococo palaces. JP

Commode
  About 1745, French
  Coromandel lacquer and ebony on oak, gilt-
    bronze mounts, *brèche d'Alep* marble top
  H. 34 in.
  Bequest of Emma A. Sheafer, The Lesley and
    Emma Sheafer Collection, 1974.356.189

Bernard Van Risenburgh (active about 1730–1765), who signed this with his initials BVRB, has been described by Sir Francis Watson as "one of the great masters of the fully developed Louis XV style." Instead of marquetry, the decoration here is colorful panels from an incised Chinese lacquer screen, skillfully adapted in Van Risenburgh's workshop to the curving front and sides. JP

Writing table
  About 1750, French
  Satiné wood, purplewood, and kingwood mar-
    quetry on oak, gilt-bronze mounts
  H. 29¾ in.
  Bequest of Emma A. Sheafer, The Lesley and
    Emma Sheafer Collection 1974.356.186

Signed by Bernard Van Risenburgh, who supplied a larger and more ornate *bureau plat* for the study of the dauphin at Versailles in 1745. A wood called *satiné*, producing an effect of watered silk, was used as a ground for the floral marquetry on both tables. JP

Corner settee
1766, German (Würzburg)
Pine, carved, painted, gilded, covered in painted oriental satin (not original)
H. 43 in.
Bequest of Emma A. Sheafer, The Lesley and Emma Sheafer Collection, 1974.356.121

Fiske Kimball traced the origins of rococo forms in Germany to French prototypes, enriched by native baroque tradition, and wrote that "their use there exceeded that in France in fantasy if not in discipline. . . . the resulting new hybrids are true and living works of art, which we see with ever growing delight." Fantasy seems to play over this extraordinary piece, part of a set of four side chairs, two armchairs, and two settees made by the cabinetmaker Johann Köhler for Seehof Castle.
JP

Long-case clock
Workshop of David Roentgen, 1741–1807, signed by Anton Reusch
Movement by Achenbach & Schidt à Neuwied
About 1785, German (Neuwied)
Oak, other woods, gilt-bronze, brass
H. 10 ft. 2½ in.
Gift of Mrs. Edgar Worch in memory of her husband, 1975.101

Mass production and international marketing of works of skilled craftsmanship, at once inventive and eclectic, was the paradox of David Roentgen, cabinetmaker and business executive. That the form of this clock resembles a Thomas Chippendale print, that the superb marquetry depicts a genre scene like no other in Roentgen's repertory, that a workman, Anton Reusch, was allowed to affix his name prominently in the marquetry, that the clock originally played an elaborate musical composition to mark the time—nothing should surprise in the production based in the small Moravian community of Neuwied, which swept the courts of Europe and numbered among its most avid clients Louis XVI and Catherine the Great.
PH

Balustrade
About 1715–1725, English
Wrought iron; cipher: Philip Stanhope, Fourth Earl of Chesterfield
H. about 35 ft.
Edward Pearce Casey Fund and funds from various donors, 65.164

Part of the grand staircase installed at Chesterfield about 1747, this belongs stylistically to the baroque tradition of ironworking. CV

Thomas Tompion
1639–1713

Table or bracket clock
  About 1700, English (London)
  Case: ebony veneer with gilded brass mounts;
    dial and movement: gilded and silvered brass
    and steel
  H. 16¼ in.
  Gift of Irwin Untermyer, 64.101.867

Tompion's fine workmanship, the ingeniousness of his designs, and the greatly improved accuracy of his timepieces, contributed vastly to the fame of English clockmaking in his era. This portable, eight-day, repeating clock is signed and numbered 269 on its splendidly engraved backplate. The repeater, a device for striking the hours in darkness, can be activated at will, while the subsidiary dial at the upper right can be used to disengage the regular striking mechanism.   cv

Probably Joseph or John Paulet

Traveling clock with calendar and alarm
  About 1700–1710, English (London)
  Silver, partly gilded, gilded brass, steel, partly
    blued
  H. 9 in.
  Gift of Irwin Untermyer, 64.101.868

In the late seventeenth and early eighteenth centuries small clocks adapted for traveling were comparatively rare. This example, in an exquisite case of engraved and repoussé silver, with a champlevé silver dial, belongs to a group of five or six examples, all signed "Paulet London." The universal ball joint at the top allows the clock to swing from its suspension ring, cushioning the jolts of motion.   cv

Ahasuerus Fromanteel
  Active about 1630–1685

Hooded wall clock with calendar
  About 1670, English (London)
  Case: ebony veneer and oak, with gilded brass
    mounts; dial and movement: gilded and
    silvered brass and steel
  H. 19½ in.
  Bequest of Irwin Untermyer, 1974.28.93

In 1658 the Fromanteel family was the first in England to adapt the newly invented Huygens pendulum, which necessitated a new form of case for the movement. The clock has an eight-day Dutch striking movement, with a short or bob pen-

dulum, and bolt and shutter maintaining power. Early English pendulum clocks were housed in wooden cases of severely architectural character. The applied Doric columns supporting the architrave and pediment of this example are of unusually pleasing proportions. CV

Seger Bombeck
German (Leipzig)

Tapestry: Augustus I of Saxony
1550
Wool, silk, metal threads
8 ft. 10½ in. x 6 ft. 1 in.
Bequest of Susan Dwight Bliss, 67.55.97

Tapestry portraits are rare. This one has the name and age of the sitter, his coat of arms, the date, and the initials of the weaver, *S. B.* (in lower right corner). EAS

Wool and silk tapestry-woven table carpet
About 1650, Dutch
5 ft. x 7 ft. 8 in.
Gift of P. A. B. Widener, 1970.250

The little unicorns in roundels in the border show that this was made to be placed on a table, with the border hanging down all around. EAS

Wool and silk tapestry: The Combat of Manricardo and Zerbino
About 1630–1650, French (Paris)
9 ft. 11 in. x 12 ft. 9 in.
Gift of Mrs. A. Exton, 1970.316

From a set illustrating Ariosto's *Orlando Furioso*. The fight between Zerbino, A Christian knight, and Manricardo, King of Tartary, is about to be stopped by the latter's lady-love, Doralice. On the right, Fiordiligi holds Orlando's horse, Brigliadoro. EAS

Robert Joseph Auguste
 About 1723–1795

Snuffbox
 1766/67, French (Paris)
 Varicolored gold
 L. 2¾ in.
 Gift of Handy and Harman, 65.255

One of only three known to have been made by Auguste, who specialized in silver tablewares (*vaisselle*). CLC

Two "spice-plates" (from a set of twelve): Abraham and Sarah Leave for Egypt; Jacob's Dream
 About 1567–1570, English (London); with the mark of Strasbourg probably struck after an assay made in the 17th c.
 Silver, parcel gilt, signed by the engraver, the monogramist "PM"
 D. 7 11/16 in.
 Gift of C. Ruxton Love, 65.260.1,8

Silver decorated entirely with pictorial engraving and intended more for display than use is the rarest of all Tudor silver. These plates may have been engraved by the Flemish master Peter Maas during a stay of several years in London as a refugee from religious persecution at home.

JMcN

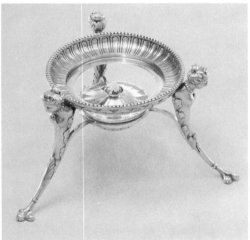

Louisa Courtauld
1729–1807

Hot-water urn
1766/67, English (London)
Silver
H. 24 3/16 in.
Gift of Madame Lilliana Teruzzi, 66.192.1

The *mouvementé* design was probably carried out by a journeyman in the shop of Samuel Courtauld, whose widow, Louisa, took over the business in 1765. The urn bears the crest of the Waterhouse family.   CLC

Firm of Matthew Boulton (1728–1809) and **John Fothergill** (about 1700–1782)

Tripod stand
1775/76, English (Birmingham)
Silver
H. 5⅛ in.
Gift of Madame Lilliana Teruzzi, 66.192.5a–c

The neoclassical elegance of this piece was probably inspired by Robert Adam's silver designs for the Soho Manufactory. The high quality of the workmanship, by an unknown craftsman, testifies to the success of the industrial organization of the Boulton and Fothergill enterprise.   CLC

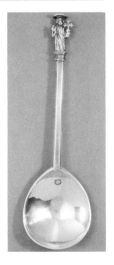

Master spoon (forming a set with eleven Apostle spoons)
1592, English (London)
Silver, figure gilded; maker's mark: crescent enclosing a W, all within a shaped shield
L. 7 3/16 in.
Gift of Mr. and Mrs. James B. Mabon, 67.166.1

With a representation of Christ, this is the "Master" spoon from one of the very few sets of sixteenth-century Apostle spoons to have survived.   JMcN

Simon Pantin
1699–1728

Kettle on Stand
1724, English (London)
Silver
H. stand 25¼ in., kettle 15½ in.
Gift of Irwin Untermyer, 68.141.81

Rarely have furniture and silver shapes been more happily combined than in this complete set of tripod table topped by a detachable salver, and the lampstand that supports a large kettle, each part distinguished by the arms or crest of the original owners, George Bowes of Streatlam Castle and Gibside, Durham, and his first wife, Eleanor. The set was made in the year of their marriage by one of London's outstanding Huguenot silversmiths.   YH

Pair of Flagons
1597, English (London)
Silver-gilt
H. 12½ in.
Gift of Irwin Untermyer, 68.141.142,143

If historical associations can enhance the meaning of works of art, it is certainly the case here. The flagons were made for Sir Edward Coke, Chief Justice of England, and for his first wife, Bridget Paston, who died in 1598. The joined arms of both, and the dates 1597 and 1598 are pricked in. Later these flagons were involved in the lawsuit concerning the Paston heirlooms, of which they formed a part until the family became extinct.   YH

Pilgrim Bottle
About 1690, English
Silver-gilt
H. 16¾ in.
Gift of Irwin Untermyer, 68.141.226

The shape is that of the traditional pilgrim bottle, made of pottery or ordinary metal and provided with a chain for submerging it in a cool stream. In England, the pilgrim bottle was revived after 1685 by French Huguenot silversmiths. The chains had by now become purely decorative, for these bottles, filled with wine, were placed in large silver cisterns.   YH

Cup with Cover
  1664, English (London)
  Silver
  H. 6⅝ in.
  Gift of Irwin Untermyer, 68.141.304

The inscription underfoot records that this cup was given by King Charles II to his Chancellor of the Exchequer, Anthony Ashley, in 1664. The royal emblems engraved on the lobed walls and cover, and the absence of hallmarks—the king was exempt from taxation on silver—reconfirm that this cup bears witness to royal taste and royal bounty.   YH

Désiré Attarge
  Died about 1878

Ewer
  1875, French (Paris); for the firm of Ferdinand
     Barbedienne (1810–1892)
  Silver-gilt
  H. 11 9/16 in.
  Rogers Fund, 69.200

Inscribed with the names of Attarge, Barbedienne, and its designer, Constant Sévin (1821–1888). Barbedienne, known for his bronze castings of sculpture, also supported a staff for the production of original work in the precious metals.
                                                    CLC

Teapot
  1870–1875, Indian, for the Anglo-Indian market
  Silver
  H. 8⅛ in.
  Gift of Marie Z. Lake, 1972.116.1–3

Part of a set that includes a sugar bowl and cream jug. The decoration combines Indian festival scenes amid palms and temples with domestic ones in European-style interiors.   CLC

Jean Baptiste Claude Odiot
1763–1850, master 1785

Teapot
About 1810, French (Paris)
Silver
H. 7¼ in.
Gift of Baroness Ida-Gro Dahlerup, 1972.226

Odiot was the foremost practitioner of this elegant, rather spare Empire style.   CLC

Jacques Nicolas Roettiers
1736–1788/89, master 1752

Vegetable dish with liner and cover
1775/76, French (Paris)
Silver
H. 7 5/16 in.
Gift of Mrs. Robert R. Livingston, 1973.318a–c

Part of a service that descended in the family of its first American owner, Chancellor Robert R. Livingston of New York (1746–1813). The design repeats several motifs used earlier by Roettiers in his "Orloff" service. The shape of the dish is unique to this service.   CLC

Marc-Etienne Janety
Active 1777–about 1812.

Sugar bowl
1786, French (Paris)
Platinum, with blue glass liner
L. 7 in.
Gift of Dr. and Mrs. A. L. Garbat, Manya Garbat Starr, and Julian A. Garbat, by exchange, and Harris Brisbane Dick Fund, 1974.164

Janety is the only Parisian silversmith known to have worked in platinum, a rare metal in his time and one difficult to use because of its high melting point. Janety's complete technical and stylistic control is evident in this bowl, believed to be the single surviving example of his work in this material.   CLC

Plate: Perseus and Andromeda
  About 1515–1520, Italian (Castel Durante)
  Tin-glazed earthenware (majolica); decorated
    by the 'In Castel Durante' painter ("Pseudo
    Pellipario")
  D. 9½ in.
  Purchase, J. Pierpont Morgan Gift, 65.6.9

Like Nicolò, whose close follower he was, the
so-called Pseudo-Pellipario used familiar woodcuts, in this case an edition of Ovid's *Metamorphoses*, published in 1497, as a source for his
compositions, combined with freer figures (such
as Andromeda), perhaps of his own design or from
a contemporary engraving.   JMcN

Plate: episode from a romance
  Signed and dated 1522, Italian (Gubbio)
  Tin-glazed earthenware (majolica): painted at
    Gubbio and lustered by Maestro Giorgio
    Andreoli; inscribed: "Me dol la infamia tua;
    piu chi morire" (Your infamy grieves me
    more than my death")
  D. 10½ in.
  Purchase, J. Pierpont Morgan Gift, 65.6.10

An example of a finely painted plate enhanced
by ruby and gold lusters, selectively applied. It
shows a particularly open composition with large
figures characteristic of early Gubbio pictorial
wares.   JMcN

Jug
  About 1460–1480, Italian (Florence)
  Tin-glazed earthenware (majolica)
  H. 16 15/16 in.
  Purchase, J. Pierpont Morgan Gift, 65.6.14

The Florentine majolica painters evolved the
pleasing diaper pattern seen here by adapting only
two of the elements—the leaves and tendrils—of
the bryony pattern so familiar to them from
imported Valencian lustered wares.

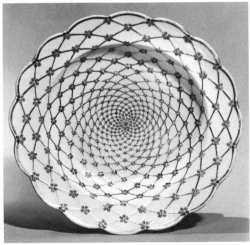

Monteith from dinner service
   About 1791, English (Staffordshire; Etruria)
   Wedgwood creamware, green, black, gilt
   D. 12¾ in.
   The Charles E. Sampson Memorial Fund, 65.30

This pleasing object with its "Water Leaf design with Green Flowers," traces both its function and its name to the deep silver bowls with notched rims that were first used in the 1680s in England for cooling wine glasses in ice water. Influenced no doubt by his large European trade, Wedgwood adopted the lower oval shape favored on the Continent.   JMcN

Mug
   1770–1773, English (Bristol)
   Hard-paste porcelain, Long Eliza pattern
   H. 4 11/16 in.
   The Charles E. Sampson Memorial Fund, 65.31

The figure decoration is a serious borrowing from Chinese porcelain decoration and not the more usual fantasized "chinoiserie" of European fabrication.   JMcN

Plate
   About 1760, Russian (St. Petersburg, Imperial
      Porcelain Manufactory)
   Hard-paste porcelain
   D. 10⅛ in.
   The Charles E. Sampson Memorial Fund, 65.47

From a dinner service made for the personal use of the Empress Elizabeth I, under whose patronage the imperial factory was firmly established.
                                                    CLC

NEXT PAGE:

Plaque: The Adoration of the Shepherds
   About 1780, Italian (Bassano)
   Terraglia inglese (creamware)
   18⅜ x 12⅝ in.
   The Charles E. Sampson Memorial Fund, 66.61

Recreates in a ceramic medium the style and subject matter of the Bassano school of painting.
                                                    JMcN

J. G. Kirchner (modeler)
　Born 1701

J. G. Heroldt (decorator)

Cup with cover and stand
　About 1728, German (Meissen)
　Hard-paste porcelain
　H. 15 9/16 in.
　Gift of R. Thornton Wilson in memory of his
　　brother, Orme Wilson, 66.63a–c

Commissioned by Augustus the Strong, Elector
of Saxony and King of Poland, to commemorate
the state visit to Dresden in January 1728 of the
king and queen of Prussia, parents of Frederick
the Great. The queen's initials, SD for Sophie-
Dorothea, are three times displayed. The larger
finial figure of Athena is closely related to a silver
statuette in the Electoral collections at Dresden,
made by Philipp Kuesel of Augsburg before 1700.
The turquoise ground has reserves with gold-lace
borders painted by Heroldt with colorful chinoiserie figures in idyllic landscapes. This splendid
cup illustrates that interesting phase of early
Meissen production when the compelling influence of all things Chinese had been superseded
by a temporary dependence on silver shapes; the
lure of the Orient continued in the painted decoration.　　　　　　　　　　　　　　　　YH

Relief portrait
　About 1770, Italian (Venice, Cozzi factory)
　Hard-paste porcelain
　H. with frame 21 in.
　Gift of R. Thornton Wilson in memory of James
　　J. Rorimer, 66.92

This relief portrait of Carlo Bertinazzi (1713–
1783), an Italian comedy actor from Turin, excells
in the sharpness and individuality of modeling.
This feat was possible in the hard white paste
used in the factory which Geminiano Cozzi
founded at Venice in 1764. The daily income of
this enterprise was safeguarded by a monopoly
on useful wares for the Venetian senate, coffee-
houses, and convents, but a few highly uncon-
ventional models had also been produced by
hitherto unidentified sculptors. One of these
might well have modeled this portrait, which
shows a close affinity with the contemporary
Venetian portraiture of Giovanni Battista Piaz-
zetta.　　　　　　　　　　　　　　　　YH

Octagonal vase
  About 1700–1710, German (Frankfurt)
  Tin-glazed earthenware
  H. 16⅞ in.
  The Charles E. Sampson Memorial Fund, 66.94

A particularly handsome example of Frankfurt faience with oriental decoration in blue, yellow, and olive green, some additional unfired red pigment, and a bold coat of arms in blue.   JMcN

Plate (from a dinner service)
  About 1750–1770, Hungarian (Holitsch)
  Tin-glazed earthenware
  D. 9½ in.
  Gift of R. Thornton Wilson in memory of Joan
    Bergère Drayton, 66.160

A very original use of the Chinese peony and hawthorne flower motifs in brilliant enamels and plentiful gilding.   JMcN

Neptune riding a seahorse
  Early 17th c., French (school of Avon)
  Earthenware with colored lead glazes
  H. 10⅜ in.
  Gift of Mrs. Francis P. Garvan, 66.236

Probably inspired by a sculpture of earlier date.
      JMcN

Rape of Proserpine
Late 18th c., Italian (probably Este)
Soft-paste porcelain
H. 19⅞ in.
The Charles E. Sampson Memorial Fund, 67.113

The movement-charged group, conceived in the round, exemplifies the sculptural bravura that sets apart the products of even the small porcelain manufactories of Italy from their counterparts elsewhere.   PH

Tureen with cover and stand
About 1765, English (Staffordshire)
Tortoiseshell ware (cream-colored earthenware with merging patches of differently colored lead glaze)
H. tureen 9 in.
The Charles E. Sampson Memorial Fund, 67.191.la,b,2

These pieces illustrate a notable aspect of Whieldon's inventive and prolific production—the creation of fine earthenwares based on contemporary silver models in dimension, form, and decoration.
                    JMcN

Bowl (from teaset)
Probably about 1758–1759, English (Lowestoft)
Soft-paste porcelain
H. 3 in.
The Charles E. Sampson Memorial Fund, 67.192.17

An example of one of the earliest patterns of the Lowestoft factory. The anonymous painter of the Chinese landscape put his number, 6, on the inside of the foot ring.   JMcN

Master Hans Resch
  Active 1563–1598

Stove tiles: The Execution of the Five Kings of the Amorites, and The Adoration of the Shepherds, with Donor
  Last quarter of 16th c., Austrian (Salzburg)
  Lead and tin-glazed earthenware
  H. 25⅝ in.
  Gift of R. Thornton Wilson in memory of Robert Francis Kennedy, 1925–1968, Senator from New York, 68.81.1,2

The elaborate tiled superstructure of stoves generally was enlarged in the sixteenth century, giving the *hofner* (stove maker) the opportunity to make larger tiles of truly pictorial composition and artistic importance. Resch is one of the few known makers of such tiles in the important center of Salzburg.   JMcN

Covered bowl
  1730, German (Meissen); mounts: about 1734, French (Paris)
  Goldsmith: Jean Ecosse (active 1705–1741)
  Hard-paste porcelain, gold mounts
  H. 4 in.
  Gift of Irwin Untermyer, 68.141.285a,b

Although porcelain has frequently been mounted in ormolu, examples set in gold are rare. This is the earliest known Meissen porcelain thus honored.   YH

Johann Joachim Kändler

Reclining goat
  About 1732, German (Meissen)
  Hard-paste porcelain
  L. 31 in.
  Purchase, Rogers Fund, 69.192

This figure, together with a group of a goat and kid, also in the Museum, was made for the gallery of the Japanese Palace at Dresden. Three groups had been completed for display by 1734, a fourth was recorded later. CLC

Cabaret
  1850–1861, French (Sèvres)
  Hard-paste porcelain
  D. 19⅝ in.
  Gift of Helen Boehm in memory of her late husband, Edward Marshall Boehm, 69.193. 1-11

The variety and delicacy of the reticulated patterns are a tour de force of skill, and it may well have been for this reason that the service was included in the *Exposition Universelle* in Paris in 1867. If the technique recalls similar work in Chinese porcelain, the shapes and decorative styles of the pieces owe almost as much to Near Eastern influence. CLC

Tile: Saint Catherine of Alexandria, from the facing of a stove in the monastic church at Goslar, built 1486
  Probably about 1486–1500, German (Lower Saxony)
  Molded and tooled earthenware decorated with colored lead glazes and some tin glaze
  12⅜ x 7⅞ in.
  Gift of R. Thornton Wilson in memory of Harriette Post Welles, 69.240

The presence of the tin glaze indicates contact of some kind between Italy and the late Gothic workshop where the tile was made. JMcN

Pair of vases: Minerva Animating Prometheus's Man of Clay; Nemesis Reading the Scroll of Fate to Jupiter

    About 1872–1882, Danish; decorated after marble reliefs by Bertel Thorwaldsen by V. Wendrich for the manufacturer, Frederick Sonne of Copenhagen

    Terracotta

    H. 8¼, 8½ in.

    Gift of Mrs. B. V. Smith, 69.216.1,2

Neoclassicism survived long in Denmark, due to Thorwaldsen's influence. His reliefs, which are the source of this vase decoration, were executed in Rome in 1810 and installed in the façade of the Palace of Christiansborg in 1825. In the last quarter of the century, vases such as these were shown in several international exhibitions, including the *Great Centennial Exhibition* in Philadelphia in 1876.   JMcN

Punch bowl

    1745–1750, China trade, for the English market

    Hard-paste porcelain

    D. 15⅜ in.

    Bequest of Alice Bradford Woolsey, 1970.212.3

The armorial, depicting Saint George trampling the French flag, was devised by the Anti-Gallican Society, an organization formed in London in 1745 to discourage the importation of French goods. This European topical motif is complemented by finely painted Chinese genre scenes enclosed in frames of Meissen derivation.   CLC

Jar

    1690–1700, China trade, for the English (?) market

    Hard-paste porcelain

    H. 8 11/16 in.

    Winfield Foundation Gift, 1970.218

The unusual way in which the leaves and flowers have been drawn suggests the original design was an embroidery. Such combinations of a religious subject with highly decorative ornament are often seen on English embroidered book covers of the mid-seventeenth century.   CLC

Giuseppe Gricci
Died 1770

A Woman and her Tailor
About 1744–1746, Italian (Capodimonte)
Soft-paste porcelain
H. 8⅛ in.
Gift of Irwin Untermyer, 1970.277.25

An early example of Capodimonte soft-paste porcelain, produced only between 1743 and 1759. Gricci derived this group from the engraving "Le Tailleur pour Femme" by Charles Cochin le Jeune. The paste is as yet somewhat impure. The colored decoration includes oriental flower motifs and a blue border recalling the stamped decoration adopted by the Ginori factory in Doccia near Florence.   YH

Mourning Virgin and Saint John
About 1743, Italian (Capodimonte)
Soft-paste porcelain
H. 15½, 18 in.
Gift of Douglas Dillon, 1971.92.1,2

Gricci, who signed the figure of the Virgin, reveals himself as a sculptor capable of creating, in the intractable medium of soft-paste porcelain, paradigms of emotive and contemplative grief.   PH

Broth bowl with cover and stand
  1793–1830, French (Apt; Moulin factory)
  Agate ware (brocatelle)
  H. without stand 5¼ in.
  Bequest of Flora E. Whiting, 1971.180.167a,b,168

The "brocatelle" ware of the Moulin factory is noted for the elegance of its forms and the refined use of the humble material—wedged clays of different colors—an improvement on the Staffordshire original. JMcN

Coffee pot
  Early 19th c., Belgian (Namur)
  Black-glazed earthenware; silver mounts probably of local manufacture; those on the lid bear French and Dutch hallmarks, reflecting the political changes of the period 1813–1815
  H. 12¼ in.
  Bequest of Flora E. Whiting, 1971.180.196a,b

Similar in shape to black-glazed English wares of the eighteenth century, this Namur piece is distinguished from them by its somewhat coarser potting. The ultimate inspiration for European black wares was Chinese "famille noire" porcelain—first imitated in Delft in the late seventeenth century. JMcN

Cup and saucer
About 1750, Italian (Doccia)
Hybrid-paste porcelain
H. cup 2 in.
The Charles E. Sampson Memorial Fund,
1971.191.1,2

This and a second cup and saucer join a teapot and sugar bowl with the same decoration acquired in 1969 and 1946. The service presents a free Italian adaptation of elements from the decorative vocabularies of the eighteenth century's leading manufactories: the yellow-ground floral panels of Meissen and the putto scenes of Sèvres. PH

Vase (one of a pair)
1792, French (Sèvres)
Hard-paste porcelain; decoration attributed to
Denis Levé (active 1754–1805)
H. 14 11/16 in.
Gift of Charles Wrightsman, 1971.206.23,24

The decoration, which evokes the French taste for oriental lacquer, is carried out in the rare combination of platinum and gold on a black ground.
CLC

Perfume burner: The Fox among the Pigeons (one of a pair)
About 1765, English (Chelsea)
Soft-paste porcelain
H. 18½ in.
Gift of Charles Wrightsman, 1971.206.25

A model produced in both the red and gold anchor periods at Chelsea but apparently in very limited numbers. The chamber for burning perfumed pastilles was in the dovecote, closed by a conical roof (now missing). JMcN

Plate
  1773, French (Sèvres)
  Gilding by Michel Barnabé Chauvaux (active
    1752–1788)
  Soft-paste porcelain
  D. 9 9/16 in.
  The Charles E. Sampson Memorial Fund,
    1972.23

The monogram is that of Charlotte Louise, wife
of Ferdinand IV of Naples. The plate was part
of a service presented to the queen, who gave
birth to a daughter in 1773, by the child's god-
father, Louis XV.   CLC

Winter
  About 1770, Italian (Doccia)
  Hybrid-paste porcelain
  H. 7¾ in.
  The Charles E. Sampson Memorial Fund,
    1972.46

The set of seasons of which this forms part were
modeled after small ivory sculptures by Balthasar
Permoser in the collection of the Ginori family,
proprietors of the Doccia porcelain manufactory.
The whereabouts of the ivories is today unknown
but the porcelain replicas survive as documents
to Permoser's power in the miniature format.
                                                     PH

Vase (vase à oignon)
  1745–1750, French (Vincennes)
  Soft-paste porcelain
  H. 6⅜ in.
  The Charles E. Sampson Memorial Fund,
    1972.132.1

This example of a model produced first at Vincennes and later at Sèvres is painted with a freshness typical of the earliest Vincennes flower work.   CLC

Table centerpiece, possibly for rosewater
  Late 18th c., Italian (Le Nove)
  Terraglia inglese (creamware)
  Modeler: possibly Domenico Bossello
  H. 14¾ in.
  The Charles E. Sampson Memorial Fund,
    1972.132.2

When discharging its function as a container for liquid, this object also completed the allusion of the decoration, two small boys perched by a pool from which one may be presumed to have filled his bottle. The playfulness and the style of the rococo survived together in Italian ceramics to the end of the eighteenth century.   JMcN

Vase
  1759, French (Sèvres)
  Soft-paste porcelain; flower painting by Vincent Taillandier
  H. 6 1/16 in.
  The Charles E. Sampson Memorial Fund,
    1972.231

Innovations in color dominate this version of the vase à oignon, with its boldly juxtaposed panels of apple green and rose. The effect is softened by the painted floral reserves and fine gold tooling.
                                        CLC

*Teapot: Callisto's Pregnancy Revealed to Diana;
The Flaying of Marsyas, based on engraved illus-
trations in an Amsterdam (1732) edition of Ovid's*
Metamorphoses
> About 1760–1770, Italian (Doccia)
> Hard-paste porcelain, relief decoration, enam-
> eled and gilded
> H. 5 11/16 in.
> The Charles E. Sampson Memorial Fund,
> 1973.134a,b

Tea and coffee services decorated in this manner
were among the Doccia factory's early productions and remained in favor far into the nineteenth century. JMcN

Dancing Girl
> About 1770, Italian (Doccia; Ginori factory)
> Soft-paste porcelain
> H. 6½ in.
> Bequest of Irwin Untermyer, 1974.28.116

J. J. Kändler
Dancing Girl
> 1748–1750, German (Meissen)
> Hard-paste porcelain
> H. 7½ in.
> Gift of Mrs. Jean Mauzé, 1974.232.1

The Meissen figure by Kändler served as model
for that made in the Ginori factory. It is fascinat-
ing to observe some of the differences that exist
between the German hard-paste figure with its
admirable sharpness of modeling, and the Italian
statuette with colors that sink into the soft-paste
like footsteps in driven snow. One might also
compare the plain base of the earlier model with
the ornate rocaille base of the later. YH

Dish
    About 1720, China trade, for the English market
    Hard-paste porcelain
    D. 12 5/16 in.
    Gift of the Winfield Foundation, Helena Wool-
        worth McCann Collection, by exchange,
        1974.195

The decoration, in a light underglaze blue, features the impaled arms of Edward Harrison
(1674–1732) and his wife, Frances Bray. The rendering of the arms by means of a few pseudo-
engraved lines and written abbreviations is believed to be unique to this service.   CLC

Plate: Joseph's Coat Shown to Isaac
    About 1560, Italian (probably Venice)
    Tin-glazed earthenware
    D. 10 13/16 in.
    Gift of Mrs. Francis P. Garvan, 1974.286

The scene is based on a woodcut in an illustrated
Bible published in Lyons in 1553 and republished
in Italian in 1554. Similar work was done in
Urbino, Pesaro, and Lyons itself. The more mea-
ger quality of the tin glaze suggests Venice as the
probable place of manufacture of this example.
                                              JMcN

Tureen and cover in shape of a blackcock
    About 1750, France (Strasbourg)
    Faience
    H. 21¼ in.
    Bequest of Emma A. Sheafer, The Lesley and
        Emma Sheafer Collection, 1974.356.237a,b

Although we ought not to judge works of art by
their size, the dimensions of this piece, as well
as its modeling and firing, represent a technical
achievement rarely attained, and only in a flour-
ishing workshop such as the one founded by Paul
Hannong in Strasbourg.   YH

Tankard
   1720–1725, German (Nuremberg)
   Faience, silver-gilt, painted with hunting
      scenes; signed M. Schmid
   H. 9¾ in.
   Bequest of Emma A. Sheafer, The Lesley and
      Emma Sheafer Collection, 1974.356.258

Schmid was among the few faience painters who
signed his work. But even without signature, his
style would be instantly recognizable, for no
other faience painter featured these bold figures
in a continuous landscape around the walls of
large tankards. Such plain shapes were ideal for
his compositions, which ignore all inhibitions or
limitations of scale that other faience painters
seem to have imposed upon themselves.   YH

Hunting cup and cover
   1741, German (Meissen)
   Hard-paste porcelain; model by J. J. Kändler
      and J. G. Ehder
   H. 15 in.
   Bequest of Emma A. Sheafer, The Lesley and
      Emma Sheafer Collection, 1974.356.337a,b

Displaying the arms of the king of Poland and
elector of Saxony, this is a splendid example of
the creativity of a modeler who derived his basic
direction from the silversmith and detailed form
from the ivory carver.   YH

Emile Gallé

Goblet
   1889, French (Nancy)
   Cameo cut, light and dark gray and brown
      mottled glass; inscribed, signed, and dated:
      "Par dessus la colline, Par dessus la vallée. . . .
      Shakespeare Nancy Emile Gallé ft Paris Ex-
      position 1889"
   H. 4⅞ in.
   Gift of Gertrude Moira Flanagan, 1972.170.1

A documentary piece recording Gallé's exhibiting
in the *Exposition Universelle* in 1889.   JMcN

*Figures from the Italian comedy: Lucinda, Donna
Martina, Isabella*
> About 1758, German (Neudeck-Nymphenburg)
> Hard-paste porcelain; models by F. A. Bustelli
> H. 7½, 7¾, 7¾ in.
> Bequest of Emma A. Sheafer, The Lesley and
>   Emma Sheafer Collection. 1974.356.802,
>   521,527

Bustelli treated his figures like actors performing
to the music of Purcell or Mozart. He knew how
to make porcelain the ideal vehicle for the creation of small sculptures, and how to impersonate
in his charades the lighthearted charm that is the
essence of rococo art.   YH

Two storage jars
   About 1620, Italy (Montelupo)
   Tin-glazed earthenware
   H. 40 in.
   The Charles E. Sampson Memorial Fund,
      1975.63.1a,b,2a,b

The only known examples of Montelupo ware with monochrome blue decoration on a near-white ground. That combination recalls the porcelain that had been the pride of Grand Duke Francesco I de' Medici in Florence. Bernardo Buontalenti was in charge of that enterprise. These large jars, therefore, represent a prolongation of that local tradition, even though the material, size, and style differ. The latter can be associated with Buontalenti's principal pupil, Giulio Parigi, who also worked for the Medici. Hence we are tempted to classify these jars as "bellissima robba a grotesche," as mentioned in the Medici account books of 1619.   YH

La Collation, from a set of eight wool and silk tapestries: Italian Village Scenes
   1762, French (Beauvais). Designed by François
      Boucher, 1736–1746; woven under the direc-
      tion of André Charlemagne Charron for the
      Boulard de Gatelier family
   H. about 9 ft. 6 in.
   Gift of Ann Payne Robertson, 64.145.3

Boucher was at the height of his powers, just back from Italy and just married, when he designed this delectable tapestry series, his first. It preserves the realism of his early works combined with the entrancing prettiness that is his outstanding characteristic. Reproducing his designs, the Beauvais manufactory, with its equally able weavers, became understandably far more popular than its solemn rival, the Gobelins. This set of the *Fêtes italiennes* is the only one of its size that has remained together, having remained in the Château de Gatellier until about 1900.

EAS

Shawl: Western-style flowers
   1850–1875, Indian, for the Western market
   Goat fleece in twill tapestry
   12 ft. 2 in. x 5 ft. 2 in.
   Rogers Fund, 65.91.2

Shawls were fashionable and often very expensive costume pieces in the nineteenth century in Europe and America. The most prized were made in northern India of the silky underfleece of the Kashmir goat in a combination of handweaving, piecing, and embroidery after pseudo-oriental designs sent out from Europe. This supreme example—entirely in the twill tapestry technique —was probably made as a special commission or for exhibition.   JM

Hanging: velvet with serpentine pomegranate design
   15th c., Spanish
   Crimson cut velvet with gold bouclé detail on
      ground of ribbed tabby with gold surface
      wefts
   9 ft. 2 in. x 5 ft. 6 in.
   Bequest of Susan Dwight Bliss, 67.55.101

Velvets patterned with this fifteenth-sixteenth century version of the palmette were named "pomegranate velvets" in the nineteenth century and have had this name ever since.   JM

Antependium: pomegranate velvet with ogival framework
   Late 15th-early 16th c., Spanish
   Pile-on-pile cut velvet on satin ground covered
      by gold surface weft; bouclé detail
   3 ft. 4 in. x 7 ft. 6 in.
   Bequest of Susan Dwight Bliss, 67.55.102

A great ornamental development of the ancient palmette motif was inseparably linked in the fifteenth and sixteenth centuries in Spain and Italy with the development of patterned velvet weaving. This particularly magnificent example of the combination appears also in a cope at the Hispanic Society.   JM

Panel of silk: palm trees, rose baskets
  Second half of 18th c., Spanish (?)
  Raspberry satin with diaper in weft floats,
    design in pattern wefts and brocading
  9 ft. 6¾ in. 3 ft. 5 in.
  Rogers Fund, 67.184.1a,b

Delightfully fanciful silks were produced for the wide-skirted dresses of the eighteenth century, especially in France and England. This one, with its naive yet striking combination of familiar and unusual motifs, does not fall into any of the established categories. Possibly it was woven in Spain, whose silk industry was revived by weavers from Lyons in the middle of the eighteenth century. JM

Length: bouquets, serpentines of lace ribbons
  1830s, English
  Cotton tabby, plate printed with resist or discharge, indigo dyed
  2 ft. 10 in. x 3 ft. 4 in.
  Rogers Fund, 67.207

The design of this unusual printed cotton is actually recorded in a series of impressions on paper in a pattern book inscribed *Fosters and Co., Bromley Hall, Middlesex, about 1780*. The technique and width of this version suggest a date in the 1830s, after discharge printing had been invented. JM

Coverlet: central medallion in field of flowers and animals; border of wool and cotton bobbin lace
  About 1800, Spanish or Mexican
  Cotton twill embroidered in brilliant crewels,
    details in couched wrapped metal thread and sequins
  7 ft. 11 in. x 4 ft. 4 in.
  Rogers Fund, 69.124

The great coverlets of the seventeenth and eighteenth centuries had their charming provincial reflections. The bulls and donkeys among brilliant flowers and sequined butterflies suggest a provenance in Catalonia or New Spain for this one. JM

Panel of "bizarre" silk
    About 1700, French or Italian
    Coral satin damask with ground pattern in weft
       face of weave; brocaded in silk and wrapped
       gold
    3 ft 7¾ in. x 1 ft. 9 in.
    Rogers Fund, 69.132.4a,b

These silks—with their extraordinary patterns in long repeats—were called "bizarre" by the Danish scholar Slomann, who believed they were made in India. Most scholars consider them an exotic phase in the history of European silk weaving.
                                      JM

Hanging: The Wayfarer Crowned by Happiness
    Third quarter of 16th c., probably northern
       French
    Wool and silk needlepoint on canvas
    8 ft. x 9 ft. 10 in.
    Bequest of Mrs. Anne Archbold, 69.298

Panels representing scenes from *The Table of Cebes,* a classical text popular during the Renaissance, on the soul's journey through life, were worked in the somber colors of northern European taste toward the end of the sixteenth century. Like another example in the collection (42.193.2), this one is based on a woodcut by David Kandel of Strasbourg.
                                        JM

Bedspread: central floral medallion, corner quarter medallions, in field of scrolling flowers and leaves
    About 1725–1750, English
    Linen embroidered with silks couched with flat
       metal strips, wrapped gold thread
    6 ft. 7 in. x 5 ft. 7 in.
    Purchase, Everfast Fabrics Inc. Gift, 1970.173

Distinguished not so much by fine stitchery as by the effectiveness of the melting shades of yellow, green, pink, and blue and the couched gold details interpreting its beautiful pattern of boldly stylized flowers and leaves.
                                        JM

Screen panel: flower sprays in side borders twined with smaller flowers
  Early 18th c., Chinese, for the French market
  Gouache-painted silk tabby
  76 x 31½ in.
  Rogers Fund, 1971.136.2

Thin silks painted with flowers, birds, and butterflies for dress lengths, fan leaves, and screen panels were the final phase of China's ancient silk trade with the West. The soft ecru ground of this unusual example, suggesting some special kind of unbleached silk, enhances the pearly quality of the white lotus and clematis petals.   JM

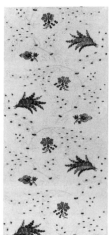

Length of white silk: curving sprays of flowers, leaves
  About 1750, English (Spitalfields)
  Silk tabby with ground pattern of large sprays in weft floats with brocaded silver foil accents enclosing small sprays brocaded in polychrome silks, silver foil, and wrapped metal thread
  4 ft. 5 in. x 1 ft. 9 in.
  Rogers Fund, 1971.136.3

Toward the middle of the eighteenth century English silks seem to have developed their own quite distinctive style—the most popular with white ground, "open and airy" designs (in the words of a contemporary author), and fresh and lively colors.   JM

Length of silk: "moresque" pattern
  1830s, French
  Satin damask with blue, cream wefts; details in various twills and weft float treatments
  7 ft. 5½ in. x 21¾ in.
  Rogers Fund, 1971.156

From the time when the Ottoman Turks restored the glory of the Eastern Empire with the conquest of Constantinople, their arabesque ornament fascinated Western designers. This intricate repeat-patterned "moresque" silk could only have been woven on a Jacquard loom of the nineteenth century, so exquisite is its curvilinear detail.   JM

Section of bed curtain: hunting scenes in floral framework

18th c., Irish

Plate-printed tabby with linen warp, cotton weft; inscribed *ROBINSON Balls Bridge*

6 ft. 6 in. x 2 ft. 5 in.

Purchase, Everfast Fabrics Inc. Gift, 1973.85

The plate-printed fabrics so popular in the second half of the eighteenth century in Europe originated in Ireland around the middle of the century. Though handsome English and French examples are numerous, surviving Irish examples, especially ones so well identified as this, are rare.

JM

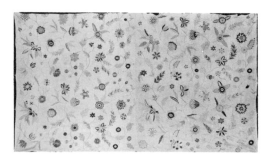

Part of a skirt with serpentines of fantastic flowers

Early 18th c., English

Linen tabby embroidered in silks in shades of blue, russet, gold

3 ft. 3½ in. x 5 ft. 6½ in.

Purchase, Everfast Fabrics, Inc. Gift, 1973.89

A traditional floral treatment takes on a new brilliance in the hands of an embroiderer who composed each small area of the elaborate repeating pattern with a different filling stitch. JM

Chasuble, maniple, stole, chalice-cover decorated with flowering sprays, birds, butterflies

Late 18th c., Chinese, for use in a Christian church

White satin embroidered with brilliant silk flosses

L. chasuble (at center back) 40 in.

Purchase, Condé Nast Publications Inc. and Everfast Fabrics Inc. Gifts, 1973.118a–d

Though Jesuit priests were received at the Chinese court with great appreciation of their learning and courtesy, a misunderstanding occurred between the Pope and Emperor K'ang-hsi toward the end of the latter's life. By the second half of the eighteenth century, Christian services were forbidden in China and vestments such as these were made only for a market outside China. JM

Skirt-front: wide front panel, deep border; field of palmettes in framework of interlacery
  About 1600, Spanish
  Ivory warp twill couched and embroidered with ivory silk yarn and cord
  H. 3 ft. 1 in.
  Rogers Fund, 1973.203

While black and white, originally Spanish court colors, were the mode all over Europe by the end of the sixteenth century, Spanish portraits support the idea that this style of skirt and the embroidered design itself are specifically Spanish.
JM

Framed picture: Jephthah greeted by his daughter and her attendants making music to celebrate his victorious return from battle
  Third quarter of 17th c., English
  Silks embroidered on linen canvas
  16¾ x 20¾ in.
  Bequest of Irwin Untermyer, 1974.28.200

This Old Testament scene was probably drawn by a local artist for the young lady of rank who worked it with unusual skill and delicacy. As was frequent, he composed the picture from a variety of sources. The graceful figures of the daughter and her attendant are seen in other embroidered pictures of the period and must have come originally from an engraving, such as the scenes from the life of David by Martin de Vos and Johann Sadler, which provided the group of Roman warriors used here to represent the elders of Gilead.
JM

Pieced and quilted coverlet
  Late 18th c., English
  Block printed and plate printed cottons (some with linen warps)
  7 ft. 10 in. x 7 ft. 7 in.
  Purchase, Rogers Fund and Springs Mills Inc. Gift, 1975.2

Pieced quilts are thought of as an American specialty, but their forerunners survive in small numbers in England, where the technique was also used for matching bed curtains. This strangely balanced arrangement of small pieces provides a cross section of French and English printed cottons of the eighteenth century, many of them not known elsewhere.
JM

Coverlet: European and Indian scenes and ornament
> 17th c., Indian (Bengal), for the Western market
> White cotton plain weave embroidered in Tussur silk
> 10 ft. 6 in. x 8 ft. 11 in.
> Gift of the Winfield Foundation, Helena Woolworth McCann Collection, by exchange, 1975.4

Teeming with episode and ornament embroidered in natural wild silk, such coverlets were famous products of Bengal long before the Portuguese introduced them into Europe in the late sixteenth century. Thereafter, European themes were mingled with Indian, as here. The flood scene in the border is from the epic of Vishnu; the Judgment of Solomon appears in the center medallion.

JM

Painted paper and ivory fan: country scenes
> About 1750, French
> H. 11½ in.
> Gift of Mrs. William Randolph Hearst, 65.80.4

The wheellike appearance of the elaborate sticks gave rise to the name "cabriolet" for fans of this rare type.   EAS

Painted paper and ivory fan: Venus and Vulcan
> About 1750, probably Dutch
> H. 10⅞ in.
> Gift of Mrs. William Randolph Hearst, 65.80.6

There are tiny, real shells in the guards of this extremely elaborate fan.   EAS

Painted paper and mother-of-pearl fan: the Battle of Sunderhausen
  1758, French
  H. 11¾ in.
  Gift of Mrs. William Randolph Hearst, 65.80.9

The Prince de Soubise, who won the battle, gallops up on the right; the defeated Hessian Prince of Isemburg slinks off on the left.   EAS